Praise fc

"In *Conscious Musings* Alexis Brooks reminds us that the perfect world we are looking for might already be here. With an emphasis on personal responsibility and the importance of service to others, we become the change we want to see. This is an intelligently written, thoughtfully composed collection of essays that examine the human potential. It is a well-researched book that examines the influence of consciousness on reality, looking at the act of reflection rather than reaction. I was particularly intrigued by the idea that a simple change in one's daily routine can be a precursor to change in other areas of life. Read this enlightening work, and as Alexis so clearly states, 'Embrace the journey'."

-William Buhlman, author of *Adventures in the Afterlife*

"*Conscious Musings* is a marvelous collection of metaphysical principles designed to both educate and enlighten the reader. I highly recommend this book."

-Dr. Bruce Goldberg, author of *Exploring the Fifth Dimension – Parallel Universes, Teleportation and Out-of-Body Travel*

"*Conscious Musings* is a celebration of inspiration and a feast for the soul. Alexis Brooks has a rare talent for combining the most mind-boggling metaphysical concepts with down-to-Earth practical ideas. She illuminates some of the great ideas of our time with graceful dexterity and takes us on a journey to comprehend the nature of reality, asking questions such as, 'Is paranormal the new normal?' *Conscious Musings* guides us through the challenges of our times, envisioning a state of mindful awareness and wonder we can attain by which all problems can be solved."

-Cynthia Sue Larson, author of *Reality Shifts – When Consciousness Changes the Physical World*

"Alexis Brooks is a great 'muser!' She zooms in on poignant topics in the news and life, and examines them in a spiritual, intuitive light. She connects the nonphysical and physical realms this way, helping us see through the veil of confusion and ignorance that surrounds us on a daily basis. It's fun to contemplate the ideas along with her. It will help you notice other important things that want noticing."

-Penney Peirce, author of *Leap of Perception* and *Frequency*

"*Conscious Musings* is wonderful, inspirational and motivating! Alexis Brooks offers insights of great depth and wisdom that she seamlessly brings together into a perfect wholeness. This book will help you gain a higher perspective on life and how to make it richer and more rewarding."

-Rosemary Ellen Guiley, author of *Dream Messages from the Afterlife* and *Soul Journeys*.

"If you are ready to contemplate the unknown, to expand your awareness, to remember who you are, I recommend *Conscious Musings* as a roadmap and Alexis Brooks your muse."

-Ann Bolinger-McQuade, author of *Everyday Oracles – Decoding the Divine Messages That Are All Around Us*

"Alexis has provided all of us with a thoughtful, beautifully written understanding of ourselves, the times we are living in and the power of love. This book is sure to inspire, motivate and stimulate our perspectives on life in an uplifting way. It is a testament to the beauty of all that we are and a beauty we should never, ever forget."

-Howard Martin, Executive Vice President, *HeartMath* and co-author with Doc Childre of *The HeartMath Solution*

"*Conscious Musings* is a deep, entertaining and enlightening journey into these times of great crisis and opportunity. Alexis Brooks effortlessly weaves personal reflections, cosmic truths, and our collective reality, into a narrative that is both thoughtful and heartful. This work is a great contribution to an awakening humanity."

-Steve Bhaerman aka Swami Beyondananda, co-author with Bruce Lipton of *Spontaneous Evolution – Our Positive Future and A Way to Get There From Here*

"Alexis Brooks' search for truth has been so diligent that her *Conscious Musings* is able to offer sophisticated insights beyond the usual platitudes. The altitude of her worldview allows her to see beyond seeming dichotomies. She describes how a true ego is necessary to be both distinct and unified with the cosmos, that responsible individualism is the core of real connectedness as community and that authentic spirituality depends on the recognition of our sovereignty of every being. Such grounded expansiveness is both inspiring and timely when both waking up and clear manifesting are critical."

-Foster Gamble, Creator of *Thrive Movie – What On Earth Will it Take?*

CONSCIOUS MUSINGS

CONSCIOUS MUSINGS

Contemplations to

Transform Life and Realize Potential

ALEXIS BROOKS

Aaron —

Continue to Embrace the

Journey.

Fondly,

Conscious Musings

Written and Edited by Alexis Brooks

This edition is revised and expanded from its original version, *Conscious Musings – A Collection of Contemplations about Life and Potentiality.*

Original release format: Spoken Word (December 2012)

ASIN: B00ATHGW42

Cover design by Justin Novelline
Cover photography by Salwa Galal/Hand Model: Alexandra Cerda
Cover concept by Alexis Brooks
Author photograph by Steven Fuld

This book includes bibliographical references.

ISBN-13: 978-0-9915250-2-7
ISBN-10: 0991525027

To all who sense the virtue in exploration, may you find truth in the beauty of one simple act – Reflection.

To Cynthia Sue Larson, my friend and kindred spirit, for encouraging this project which culminated in a true 'labor of love.' I wouldn't have written this book without you!

To my confidant in all things wondrous, mysterious and just plain fascinating – Sahar, you are the sister I never had!

To Nancy "Mom Suzy" Wilson, you've given the world the gift of your song, but you've given me the immeasurable gift of family! Thanks for enduring countless hours of my jaunts into stories of the "unusual" and for sharing a few of your own with me!

To my mother and father, who nurtured my inquisitive character, though your physical presence may be absent from my sight, your eternal presence is alive in my heart.

AND

To Derek
For being with me step-by-step on this incredible journey and for helping me to see the unlimited potential in all things.
I simply Love you!

"…I had to abandon the idea of the superordinate position of the ego. After all, I had been brought up short when I had attempted to maintain it…I saw that everything, all paths I had been following, all steps I had taken, were leading back to a single point – namely to the midpoint. It became increasingly plain to me that the mandala is the center. It is the exponent of all paths. It is the path to the center, individuation.

…I began to understand that the goal of psychic development is the self. There is no linear evolution; there is only a circumambulation of the self."

- C.G. Jung, Memories, Dreams, Reflections

CONTENTS

SECTION THREE
THE CONSCIOUSNESS OF MANIFESTATION & ABUNDANCE

INTRODUCTION
❧ ❦

S tay with me because we are about to take a thrill ride! *Conscious Musings* is a journey down reality highway – a true investigation into the nature of self, our world, and our potential.

But first, let's have a reality check...

Few would argue that the world that we currently experience leaves much to be desired. True happiness is too often traded in for survival and average content; creativity for everyday acquired skills – like a job that we do not because we like it, but because we were trained for it. Many believe that's all that life has to offer. I am here to tell you that is simply not so!

Did something along the path of our evolution of becoming modern man somehow thwart or throw us off track from realizing how absolutely powerful, creative, and limitless we are as human and spiritual beings? Will there one day be a collective realization of these things?

The following essays will begin by taking an honest and critical look at society, human personality, and the current state of our world. I feel strongly that one must use unbiased introspection to realize where we are in our growth and evolution in order to root out the challenges and begin the process of embodying the solutions. This can be done both individually and collectively.

It cannot be said too often. *We* are the change we've been waiting for! You'll hear me say that quite often throughout this book. The moment we acknowledge this and put positive change into practice, we will see the light shining brightly for us at the end of the tunnel and the pot of gold at the end of the rainbow.

We have now passed the well documented and meticulously calculated turning point of December 21, 2012 and I suppose many of you are asking, *what happened?* Unfortunately, countless individuals were primed through a continuum of messages to expect some acute transition on this fated day. Perhaps you were delighted that the world didn't end with a massive landslide or a multi-continent tsunami or get plummeted by a giant meteor. Maybe you were anxiously anticipating this revelatory moment to elicit the immediate birthing of a new consciousness, an instant annihilation of the systems and institutions that have kept us on lock down for millennia, and a giant gate of salvation to be opened for all to enter. Looking through our physical eyes, it appears that none of this has happened. And yet a subtle and purposeful shift which I still feel to be underway, has gently nudged many of us toward the need to look deeper, beyond what the physical eyes can process.

With this *inner perception,* we are finally beginning to realize that we must change ourselves in order to change our world. Conceivably, this is what this date and the dates preceding and succeeding December 21, 2012 all mean.

For sure, the Universe is speaking to us and while in the midst of this *shift,* its ways and means seem to be expanding greatly – the urgency to get the message across magnified multifold! In this collection of essays we will take a look at these very ways and means; the spectrum of reality that is changing, increasing, and lifting its veil to reveal to us that *this shift is real!*

But first, we must examine where we've come from and where we are, in order to have a sense as to where we are going.

In the opening section, *The Individual, the Collective, and Social Consciousness*, we will examine our current psychological state amid the common construct we find ourselves in. Fair warning – I will not spare you dear reader, with a comfy-cozy picture seen through rose colored glasses. The musings here depict the world as it is experienced in consensus; how we've been habituated toward a very fixed and unrelenting view of reality, despite the cornucopia of history, data, and experience that has revealed anything but! We will examine how choice can free us from the grip of compliance, how ego has been over-stimulated through modern culture, how true revolution will be achieved only through personal and unconditional *evolution,* and how ultimately we have forfeited our power in favor of outside authority dictating what is possible in our lives and in the lives of others. We'll look at the individual vs. the collective, the wide swings of consciousness that co-exist in this matrix of the physical world and the consequences of resistance to change.

Once we've digested the initial *bitter pill,* we will go a bit deeper into the labyrinth of paranormal experience and why so many deny the reality of these encounters; that which has been broadly framed as mystical when in actuality, the focus on such matters may be the key to understanding our own potentiality and reality-at-large. A few of these pieces take on a more "journalistic" feel, providing documented anecdotes which lend infallible evidence to the pervasiveness of the phenomenon of extraordinary or paranormal experience. With such persistence of phenomena written within the annals of our human story, it would be difficult to ignore its relevance to the understanding of our reality and how we operate within it!

In this controversial but revealing section entitled, *The Magic, Mystery, and Metaphysics of Potentiality,* we will unravel the mystery of extraordinary experience to everyday people on a broader scale, muse the subject of reincarnation and past lives of both humans and our animal companions – and how the evidence of such a phenomenon may hold yet another key to our enlightenment while in *this* life. We will journey beyond the physical to reveal a variety of experiences that can be achieved in the out-of-body (OBE) state and examine the intersection of corporeal and non-corporeal as part of our everyday lives.

The big question – in this *post 2012 world*, can we afford to continue to ignore these phenomena that we so commonly describe as paranormal? The intimations of an immense reality are knocking on our door to help usher us through this shift and into a new world, *only* if we so choose!

In the final section, *The Consciousness of Manifestation and Abundance,* I invite you the reader, the explorer, the experiencer, to journey with me through the terrain of possibility. I encourage you to consider putting aside your previously held *beliefs* about how reality creation and manifestation work and commit to taking on a new process for creating you and the world around you. These are not original musings, but the delivery is uniquely suited to the context of this discourse.

I conclude with a transformational footnote from which I can personally attest – my own unexpected journey and the manifestation that resulted from it *after* this book had been written!

This is what I'll call the *productive* side of Conscious Musings. After pounding the pavement with a life review of the world as it is, let us now take a look at the world as it could be, but let us take it out of the possible and into the *actionable!* How refreshing it is to know that the world as it could be is indeed at our doorstep...all because we *are* in the midst of this shift. Exciting things are happening. The Universe is supporting us in every way possible. Reality creation is just not as hard as it used to be. But be careful because if we create our reality by our thoughts, emotions, and actions, whatever state we find ourselves in these days might just boomerang a mirrored reality right back to us in an instant! This is what can happen when the veil lifts, the frequency increases and the shift percolates with unabashed fervor.

This book is not designed to be a long and laborious read. I have kept it rather short with an objective in mind. My intent is to convey these very crucial contemplations to you the reader, then request that you close the book and begin your own contemplative journey which can guide you toward seeing life with new eyes!

So let's ride the waves of Conscious Musings together and discover the new world that is genuinely right in our midst. Then discover the true gems of life and potential that we've desired for so long!

SECTION ONE

THE INDIVIDUAL, THE COLLECTIVE & SOCIAL CONSCIOUSNESS

To examine the human psyche and its trajectory along an historical path laden with misunderstanding, delusion, and confined ideologies of the world and of self, one would think that there is no hope for mankind to transcend his limits and become anything more than the fractional being he's so readily accepted.

When you simply look around you and you see evidence of an increasingly unaware society – unaware of the power inherent within us all, it is impossible not to acknowledge this state of affairs with absolute concern. However, many are not *looking* at all. Instead they are too busy consuming reality as it is conveyed to them, no questions asked.

In this twenty-first century, so many have relied on the consensus picture beamed daily from our ever expanding TV screens and ever shrinking devices. Not all, but still far too many are absolutely oblivious to a world outside of these frame-by-frame images and resist un-tethering themselves from the convenience of a projected reality while relinquishing their right to explore outside of the electrical matrix. As a result, the psyche has become unquestioning and complacent!

How did this happen? How did we get here? And is there any prospect of one day reversing the trajectory, hitting the reset button and starting with a fresh, new perspective – this time with full awareness of who we once were – powerful, creative, intuitive, and limitless beings?

I do think so. But in order to ignite this next phase in our development, I feel it is absolutely necessary to deconstruct our immediate "past" and "present," take a good long objective look at ourselves – this time without the lenses of consensus and belief, shake our heads in acknowledgement and compassion, then immediately adopt a sense of urgency to re-

member who we really are.

In this first essay, entitled *Dichotomy of Consciousness and the Precipice of Change,* you will have an opportunity to contemplate our choice point in history; that point on the evolutionary scale that we find ourselves in, and make a decision to move the needle in whatever direction you find appropriate. The time is certainly *now* to contemplate, assimilate, and then take responsibility for the world that we inhabit and the lives that we lead!

"Every man must decide whether he will walk in the light of creative altruism or in the darkness of destructive selfishness."
-Martin Luther King, Jr.

One

Dichotomy of Consciousness & the Precipice of Change

I recall waxing philosophical many years ago with a friend about the prospect of one day seeing a world where extreme opposites will co-exist; where humans will engage in the worst of behavior and the best. Apathy will sit side by side with empathy, greed with giving, and so on. But then we reasoned, just as the darkest times are usually an indicator of the birth of a brighter day, such will be the case when the dichotomy of consciousness reaches its peak.

It is rather poignant that as I sit here right now, contemplating the apparent duality of human behavior, I am peering out of my window noticing how nature mirrors those very characteristics. The thunder is roaring with an angry growl, the rains are pouring and beating down on the house with a fury, while simultaneously the sun is visibly shining above it all! This is what I am observing right now as I jot these *musings* – both literally and metaphorically!

In southern folklore, when a sun-shower occurs, it is said that "the devil is beating his wife." One could infer from this saying that two opposites are co-existing – one side representing the wicked aggressor, the other representing the more innocent and benevolent. Regardless of the origin or philosophy from which this saying springs, the timing of this natural display spoke to me deeply!

Such is the *climate* for which we are currently immersed.

From my own purview, as both an entrepreneur in the sterile business world and writer within the *new thought* space, I have seen a steady escalation of competition, cognitive dissonance, ignorance, and apathy. And yet within the same framework, a movement of awakening, freedom, generosity, and cooperation have also accelerated. Indeed, darkness and light are sharing the same space!

Action and Non-Action

Within this very space we have seen the recent proliferation of various occupy movements; groups of fiercely committed citizens, who have roused to the idea that our freedoms have been hijacked and the behavior of our legacy institutions will no longer be tolerated. Initially this was seen as a protest in a vacuum, but then it quickly spread, dotting the land, gaining momentum with emotional equity and commitment to the point where it could no longer be ignored. Concurrently, there seems to be an epidemic of people wallowing in the coma of complacency, disconnected from their surroundings, cocooned in a comfort zone of day-to-day life and oblivious to any prospect of anything beyond what they normally see and do.

Shortly after the 9/11 events, I published an article called *Victims of the Attack – Martyrs for Meaning* in which I quoted noted author PMH Atwater. In it she said: "[This event represented] a wake-up call [that] was needed – one horrendous enough to reverberate across our country and the globe, affecting every man, woman, and child and in every nation. Many are those who have grown complacent in life – sloppy of dress, rigid in beliefs, uncaring in the consequences of personal activities, ever needful of another addiction convincing enough to prove we are alive…The people who died sacrificed their lives to make the statement that none of us can continue to live the way we have. It is time to awaken...Our complacency comes from putting 'things' ahead of service and investment; a consumerism gone mad, a spirituality deemed little more than new age nonsense."

Hard to believe that this reflection was penned over a decade ago and is still holding true for many. And yet, in the years since that significant day, many have boldly made the choice to stand on the side of the dichotomy that denotes purpose, intention and action; willing to shed their former selves, in order to create anew.

Service to Self vs. Service to Others

The lines of demarcation have yet to blur when it comes to the seemingly intractable dichotomy of service to self vs. service to others.

During this choice point in our history, many have remained faithful to a fear-laden mentality that is based on survival. Competition to win for one's own sake takes precedence over cooperation and team effort for the overall victory. Certainly our external channels of information that signal what our normal behavior should be – namely our mainstream media – makes for a template of self service that many have become accustomed to.

In spite of the incessant messages of survival that threaten to corral our consciousness on a daily basis, there is a sense on the part of others that selflessness will be central to transforming the future of this planet. It is fortunate that we are seeing acts of kindness multiply in the most creative ways.

I recently learned of a unique project called *The Bank of Happiness*. The bank was designed as a portal for good deeds where individuals are invited to deposit acts of kindness and others can withdraw from the depository, depending on their need, free of charge! It could be someone who is seeking a teacher to learn to speak English fluently or an offer to listen to a stranger's problems. Others have offered financial counseling, IT consulting and even dog walking! The online portal, created in 2008 by Airi Kivi, an Estonian-based psychologist states, "We were inspired by the clear understanding that there is a gap in the society between humane caring and economic well-being... We were then and are today convinced that the formula of happiness lies in noticing others. We feel that people want to help others, but often don't know how." As of this writing, *The Bank of Happiness* has over 2,000 users from Estonia as well as other countries around the globe.

The very act of altruism – lending a hand to help another without expectation of a return favor demonstrates that service to others nets a gratifying experience that ultimately serves to warm the heart of the self! Thus, service to others *is* service to self!

The fact that we have reached this dichotomy of consciousness may be a blessing in disguise; an opportunity to choose which side of the dichotomy we wish to be a part of, or better yet, use our powers of transformation to blur the lines of opposites altogether. We ultimately have choice – we always have! Choice to live by status quo ideologies or not to conform at all, choice to see and experience the wonder of life or feel as if we are a victim of it, choice to adopt what we are told or choice to question it – choice to stay the same or choice to change.

Despite the grip of a fixed world view; a maze of messages designed to inhibit our potential, a more fluid and dynamic tone is emerging, and once we choose to hear that tone we will be able to look at the dichotomy in the rear view mirror and leave the polarities behind.

"In a paradox, opposites do not negate each other – they cohere in the mysterious unity at the heart of reality."

-Parker Palmer

As I reflect on the sun-shower synchronicity while in the middle of writing this piece, I am also reminded of nature's miracles that result from such a confluence. Rainbows are a common result when rain and sun co-exist, a blending and blurring of colors within the visible spectrum of light, like the polarities – dichotomies that may soon blur as we reach the threshold of this new world.

We are in the midst of a collection of years; a time period that is nudging us to realize that we are indeed on the precipice of realizing our potential. Throughout the course of this shift, the question will persist: Will you expand or repress consciousness? By committing to divorcing from the cacophony of the current world and joining the new, we will become the change we've been so longing to see!

"When fear dissipates, change becomes a pleasurable digression."
-The Author

Two

❧ ❧

EXPERIENCING THE TURNING POINT
TREPIDATION OR TRANSFORMATION?

Now that we have acknowledged this dichotomy of consciousness, we must consider the prospect that we are on the verge of an apocalypse. The existence of drastic climate change, economic meltdown, the gradual but certain crumbling of nearly every system we've held near and dear to us for generations, are all very real. Seemingly insurmountable challenges are duking it out with larger than life opportunities – and the challenges appear to be going the full distance, repeatedly getting up with inexhaustible energy. The direction seems obvious. Or does it?

First off, when we use the term "apocalypse," many assume its singular definition as one of disaster, destruction, the end. Not true. Apocalypse also means the revealing, the uncovering. But uncovering of what?

The supposed ending of the Mayan calendar, December 21, 2012, provided the impetus for widespread chatter and often deleterious influence, led by Hollywood, the media, and the Internet – somehow deciding that the consequence of this rare galactic alignment equaled catastrophe. Certainly, we have since seen this was not the case. But when a message and its inferences become redundant and in an age where news travels in a nanosecond, belief is apt to be adopted as unanimity and quickly. Couple that with the absolute insanity we are seeing around us: the steady escalation of junk news and views, the hyperactivity of consumerism and the growing polarity, pitting people against each other on every conceivable topic – and it seems as though something absolutely horrible is all but certain. In this post-2012 era, let us still consider that if indeed we are on the edge of an uncovering – a revealing of some sort, what is to be exposed may very well transform human kind in ways that were heretofore unimaginable. Maybe we are about to experience the tipping point of a collective shift that will allow man to finally be who and what he was truly meant to be – and maybe there is a movement to ensure that this does not happen, hence the desperate attempt to keep us deaf, dumb and distracted with a *catastrophobic* version of the future.

I for one, have always been a proponent of consciousness creating reality as opposed to reality creating us ergo, *if* we decide that what we are tuning into; the white noise jumping out of the media machine and into our heads is real, certainly we are adding fuel to the fire of catastrophe by helping to set up the template for creating *that* reality. The emotional result will net absolute trepidation and the opportunity to transform, greatly diminished.

Many have confused information with *wisdom*, never considering that the "information" may belie the truth. If we are to properly navigate this shift responsibility, discrimination and independent thinking must take precedence!

In *The Mystery of 2012 – Predictions, Prophecies and Possibilities*, acclaimed author and contributor Peter Russell writes, "At this point, the growth rate of human knowledge will be reaching its own maximum…knowledge is not the end point of the evolution of intelligence. Many have pointed to a hierarchy of data, information, knowledge, and wisdom. Information can be defined as the patterns extracted from raw data. Knowledge is the generalization of information to other situations.

Wisdom determines how that knowledge is used. It involves discernment and evaluation...At present, humanity has vast amounts of knowledge, but still very little wisdom. Without developing wisdom, it is most unlikely that we will avoid catastrophe."

We are being presented with the opportunity to transform, but with this one obvious caveat as Russell so succinctly points out.

Trepidation provides a common stencil, carved out for us all too often. In light of what mankind is facing during these supposed *apocalyptic* times – that fear is in the driver's seat, it is little wonder. But as alchemists, which I believe us all to be at our core; we have the ability to transform fear, angst and concern into love, calm and compassion from the moment we realize we have the freedom to do so!

Free will is the ability to make choices without any intervention or any pre-set belief system imposing its prototype on us. Appearances can be deceiving. Let us go beyond the appearances of what seems to be and commit to choosing from a point of insight and wisdom and the revealing of something grand is sure to meet us half way.

"To become wholly compassionate requires us to open our eyes and hearts, to behold the pain and exploitation our culture obscures, to arouse deadened emotions, and to rise above our egos."
-Joanne Stepaniak

Three

❦ ❧

DEATH OF THE EGO – R.I.P.

In the midst of all this dichotomy busting, polarity blurring, and drastic transformation, just when you think you've seen it all, you wake up, turn on your TV, and glimpse the following...

> **BREAKING NEWS** – *Well known for its leadership, direction and often insatiable appetite for attention; worshipped by millions, perhaps billions the world over, the Ego was found dead just a few short hours ago. The cause is unknown. Details are still unfolding. Stay tuned as we follow this shocking and unexpected breaking news story.*

Of course if this were a *real* scenario, no doubt the mainstream media would report this astounding revelation with stupendous surprise and bewilderment. How could something so central to the human experience; that which has lived at least as long as man himself and was thought to be indestructible, perish in an instant? The bedrock of motivation that has catapulted many from a meager existence of anonymity to exulted states of power if but only *perceived* representations of power – the ego has been the initiator, the motivator, the protector for millennia.

Remember this infamous line from a commercial for Monster.com? *"When I grow up – I wanna claw my way up to middle management..."* Or this, from the original movie, Wall Street:

"The point is, ladies and gentlemen that greed, for lack of a better word – is good. Greed is right. Greed works…"

Juxtaposing these two very telling statements that have been ingested by large throngs of television watching and movie going people, you might think that each represents an opposing image of self; that of the parody mirroring the hopeless workforce expecting to achieve mere mediocrity at best, and that of the narcissistic businessman who takes no pains in paining others for his own personal gain. One will manage survival, the other material excess. And yet, these two archetypes share common characteristics – an allegiance to the part of the human physiology and psychology we call the "left brain."

We know that the brain is a complex organ that still eludes even the best in neuroscience. A numinous and anomalous part of the anatomy, many scientists acknowledge that there is much yet to know about its function and capacity as it relates to the overall structure of the human genome. In my essay, *How to Manifest – Let's Get to the Heart of the Matter* which we will explore later in this book, we look at the discoveries having to do with the energetic frequencies of the heart. It has been found that the heart generates potency far beyond that of the brain. But moreover, the alignment of the heart with the brain allows for a coherence to occur, thereby giving the brain a starring role in this process as well.

But what happened along the line of man's evolution that the brain – and in particular, that of the left-hemisphere of the brain which is said to house attributes commonly known as "the ego" – became strangely over-developed and perpetually dominated the whole of the neurological structure and psyche of man?

Many ancient and indigenous traditions recognized that

reality is in truth seamless and consciousness is a continuum of experience, thereby making it useless to compartmentalize the elements of the brain. In fact, theirs was about true integration of heart and brain to activate a sensory experience – whereby achieving a purview of the vast spectrum of reality both physical and nonphysical. What ego loves to do is resist this continuum and divorce itself from its partner, the intuition; that aspect that is more naturally linked to the heart. The ego feels it necessary to exert authority over intuition – scolding it for occasionally raising its hand to say, "Hey, I have a better idea!"

The late great scholar, thinker, and philosopher Terence McKenna spoke of the bifurcation of experience, relegating this to the lower dimensions. He contrasted the experience of synchronicity as an occurrence where ego takes a back seat. "(Synchronicity is) a curious juxtaposition of a psychic event like the thought of an old friend and an event in the so-called exterior world, such as the old friend suddenly calling on the telephone – so that it gives the impression that psyche and world are somehow contiguous with each other."

McKenna was well known for his exotic excursions; traveling to remote locations where shamanic cultures have for many years experimented with hallucinogenic plants in order to trigger an inner journey that catapulted them into multidimensional experiences of reality. He delineates these cultures from our own, in which reality both internal and external are but one sequence of experience that cannot actually be divided or separated, save for our own interpretation of it. He says, "The ego is the great boundary definer, the great divider of phenomena and it's a kind of a necessary evil. The ego is like a calcareous tumor that begins to grow in the structure of the psyche when there is not repeated contact with the kind of boundary dissolving ecstasy that traditional 'preliterate' tribes-people have built into their societies through the institution of shamanism and through the institution of group use of psychedelic plants."

He goes on, "History is a kind of descent into a lower dimension where everything is seen through the distorting lens of the ego. What we will then lack is the cohesiveness of mind." This then intimates that whether taking shamanic plants to experience true left-right brain integration or to simply recognize and choose to experience reality as a seamless whole, this is the more preferred state to activate a fuller reality.

Where I think many of us understand and even agree with this process, if only on an intellectual level and occasionally on an *instinctual* level, there is still this subtle resistance to migrate fully from the service of the ego because it has become so ingrained into our daily lives.

As children we vie for attention from our parents. We want what we want – because *we want it.* We grow through adolescence and into adulthood with the same basic needs of want: we want to be needed, we want to be heard, we want to be loved, we want to be appreciated. And then there are the basic instincts associated with the ego, given that the world we've developed is predicated on defending one's self. We need to be vigilant, we need to be guarded, we need to protect ourselves, etc. This denotes a function of an overstimulated state of *fear* and the need to survive. This is what McKenna means when he says ego is a kind of necessary evil.

The point is to not scold ourselves for this primary function that at times serves good purpose, relative to circumstances that seem thrust upon us, but to simply recognize this inherent quality as one that clearly became too overstimulated amid our human development.

On occasion, I have had to step out of myself and look

objectively at my behavior, benign as it may have appeared, to recognize that certain things I might have said or the way I might have behaved was truly a function of ego and nothing more.

But rather than hang my head in shame, I've learned that by simply acknowledging how habitual our egoistic aspects are, we may over time eventually fade its dominance from our daily reality and allow the *right side* to take its proper place of prominence.

It seems rather evident that we are living at a time when the planet is experiencing a ramping up of energetic frequencies and that a true synthesizing of both left and right (ego and intuition) are necessary to integrate this *upgrading* of energy. If we draw a correlation of the patterns in nature as being a macrocosmic representation of ourselves – the *micro*, and we know that nature is fundamentally cooperative wherein all of its constituents work in tandem rather than apart from one another to achieve its full potential, then we can deduce that this process is our natural state as well and one that would better serve us. Here we see a perfect syllogism playing out.

Mere recognition of this inherent pattern may be just the formula to begin to get the ego to *rest in peace*. For we are not speaking of the annihilation of the ego per se, but rather the true integration of left and right, spawning a blurring of polarity at every level – physical, psychological, spiritual and so on.

I do not anticipate getting such *breaking news* as that which we hypothesized at the open of this piece, but what I do truly sense is a call for the mass awakening of consciousness; a collective realization that experience is but one seamless journey of exploration and that each of us, as separate as we *appear* to be, are but a multitude of expressions of a continuum of reality. The ego is a primal part of the human experience, but as nature seeks balance, we too must seek to bring our selves back to equilibrium in order to activate the fullness of life that has been patiently waiting to present itself to the whole of mankind.

When we speak of a continuum of reality and consciousness, let us not forget that we do have identity; uniquely representing a grand field of awareness, seeking to express itself in a variety of ways. In the next essay, we'll explore the role of the individual in this grand field and why it is imperative that we embrace the unconditional distinctiveness of ourselves in this new world.

"Most people are other people. Their thoughts are someone else's opinions, their lives a mimicry, their passions a quotation."
-Oscar Wilde

Four

❧ ❧

THE EMERGENCE OF INDIVIDUALISM

My life is its own definition. So is yours.
Let us leave the priests to their hells and heavens, and confine the scientists
to their dying universe, with its accidentally created stars. Let us each dare
to open our dream's door, and
explore the unofficial thresholds, where we begin.

-'A Psychic Manifesto' by Jane Roberts

Sometime ago, I was having a discussion with an employee of a company from whom our small business had just been awarded a "plum contract." I had a couple of simple questions for him relative to the public relations surrounding our recent win, of which I had asked him to weigh in on the award for an upcoming press release. He quickly cut me off and said, "I am not *allowed* to have anything to do with such a request. I only do as I'm told…"

As an entrepreneur wearing two hats, both as independent writer and marketing executive for our small business, I've been fortunate that I've not been in a position where conformity to corporate rules was inescapable.

Frankly, I've always questioned the need to conform to what we call social consent at all, feeling on some level that mass thought and the ideas that preoccupy the collective mind are but a relative notion at best. It's a complicated issue I suppose. As human beings; biological creatures of belief and habit, our inevitable trajectory from birth thrusts us into a world of assumptions, albeit presented as facts. Our parents, our teachers, well meaning as they may be, and all the systems that proclaim "authority" engenders a perception that their truth is *the* truth and therefore it is needless to question. When these "truths" are disseminated and repeated on a grand scale, coming from our sciences, religions, history, etc., through redundancy alone, or with the assumption that there are no other choices to create from, they become adopted by the mind as actuality.

We've all heard the popular, although now clichéd phrase "think outside of the box" – upon reflection, one can deduce that reality has been largely *packaged.* But with all its bows and ribbons, as neatly wrapped as this box may be, it's not the only present under the tree. In fact, my husband and I have our own phrase of which we say often: "There is no box" – sort of Zen in its approach, although instinctively appropriate.

Groupthink

A term first popularized by William H. Whyte, Jr., who in 1952 wrote an article in Fortune magazine in which he said, "Groupthink being a coinage – and, admittedly, a loaded one – a working definition is in order. We are not talking about mere instinctive conformity – it is, after all, a perennial failing of mankind. What we are talking about is a rationalized conformity – an open, articulate philosophy which holds that group values are not only expedient but right and good as well."

Groupthink or consensus ideology has domineered its way not only into the corporate world, but in virtually all aspects of modern life. As writer and philosopher Neil Kramer stated in his essay, *The Path of One,* "Collectivism is rewarded over independence; compliance over distinctiveness." And so, if one seeks reward in one's life, one must conform to collectivism.

I'm not going to get into the unraveling of the philosophy behind group-mind or the myriad examples of how this matrix of reality has lured the masses into a collective thinking pattern – I'm sure many of you have reasoned out its framework on your own. Rather, let's look at why now more than ever, we must awaken to our individuality in order to understand, interact with, and benefit from an infinite spectrum of experience gleaned largely from our individuality.

The Paradox of the Collective and the Individual

Noted physicist David Bohm famously postulated a metaphor about the individual and the collective, liking individuals to whirlpools in a stream. Bohm reasoned that, as you look at little whirlpools forming in a body of water, it is impossible to abstract out the whirlpools from the water. They are part of the continuum of the stream and therefore part of the whole. Like whirlpools, "we are beings without borders, we are a continuum of everything else (and therefore part of the collective), but that doesn't take away from our uniqueness. We have identity; we just don't have distinct borders."

This analogy, although paradoxical as it may be to our discussion here, is pertinent nonetheless in elucidating the subtleties of the "we are all connected" vs. the "I am an individual," mindset. The fact is that both are true. But it is in the understanding and supporting of our individualism – our uniqueness, including and especially our thought processes; that which we have always had total freedom in shaping for ourselves, that can free us from the grip of *groupthink*. This understanding may be what is needed to bootstrap us out of the proverbial *box* and into a Universe that is far more fluid, intelligent and infinite than we could have ever imagined.

That said, it is indeed beneficial to appreciate our interconnectedness to each other – to all things in fact. In so doing, we will begin to create new rules of reality, ascertain greater wisdom from each other, from nature, and from the Universe. And now, as we appear to be on the threshold of a planetary shift in consciousness, *groupthink* just won't do!

Fortunately, the shift that is occurring before our very eyes and souls has yielded an awakening for some – a recognition that individual discernment is necessary to evolve. Free and unencumbered thought and feeling are innate faculties. Nonetheless, far too many are still adhering to the old pattern of group thought. In order to go with the shift, we must shake off our previously fed concepts of what "is" or "isn't," stare consensus in the face and say, "I will determine what is true, real and noteworthy." This is where real reward begins to reveal itself.

"Society everywhere is in conspiracy against the manhood of every one of its members. Society is a joint-stock company, in which the members agree, for the better securing of his bread to each shareholder, to surrender the liberty and culture of the eater. The virtue in most request is conformity. Self-reliance is its aversion."

-'Self Reliance' by Ralph Waldo Emerson

As daunting as it may seem, given the social, cultural and political fortifications that have habituated man toward a fixed worldview, it is imperative that we re-examine, question, and thus reshape what it is we believe and proudly but humbly exert our individuality in the process. Then we will no longer be doing "what we're told" but living *who we are*!

"I believe that whatever you believe in opens the door on that reality."
-Michael Talbot

Five

❧ ❧

RATIONALIZING REALITY

Collectivism has a peculiar habit of yielding the mimicking of behaviors and language. Once an expression is adopted by some, it seems uncanny how quickly it can spread into the societal vernacular. Let us now take a look at how mass expression can lead to shaping our own reality, especially when they are repeated without full awareness of the ramifications that can play out in our lives.

~~~

Casual discourse can be strangely revealing. Those informal conversations we have every day, make known intimations of the plight of our neighbor, our co-worker, our family member or friend. "Life *is* what it *is*," "I can't complain," "Things could be worse."

Phrases that are rife and recorded in our modern lexicon of life leave clues as to the shared reality most have agreed to experience and moreover, never question.

The materialist's view of reality is one that is fixed and immutable. And so it is useless to change a paradigm that is frozen and unyielding. Woe is he who kicks the structure of reality, only to get his toes bruised. At least that's what he thinks. He is joined by many others who not only defend the consensus, but are completely oblivious to any alternative.

Nonetheless, knowledge of the plasticity of reality has managed to bleed its way into the cracks of our societal edifice. Our ancient traditions; enlightened civilizations pre-dating our own have told us through time immemorial that reality is but a construct and one that can be deconstructed and rebuilt at will, both individually and en masse. In Hinduism, reality is *Maya*, roughly defined as *illusion*. And yet, despite the adamancy and continuity of this message, most resist embracing this perennial philosophy and simply settle in rationalizing their reality as if surrendering to its supposed immutable laws.

The late author and researcher Michael Talbot gives an impressive illustration as to the plasticity of reality as explained in his book *The Holographic Universe*. Talbot conveys a first person account in which his father had invited over a friend for a social gathering, who was both hypnotist and magician. Talbot being present at this event, watched as the gentleman proceeded to put one of the party guests into a hypnotic state and then told him that when he came out of his state, he would no longer be able to see his daughter in the room. On command, the man awakened, daughter in plain sight to everyone except her father. The hypnotist asked if he could see the girl anywhere in the room. He then scanned the room, wall to wall but did not see his daughter anywhere. Of course the other guests were amused at this but the father insisted he could not see the girl, despite her blatant presence directly in front of him. The hypnotist then took a pocket watch and placed it at the small of the little girl's back and then asked the man if he could see what he was holding in his hand. The man leaned forward slightly – peering seemingly through the little girl's back and said, "you're holding a pocket watch." He was then asked to read the inscription on the watch and did so with absolutely no visual impediment. With this illustration, Talbot reminds us that reality leaves clues as to its illusory nature.

Shamanic journeying is a process by which an individual or group of individuals go into altered states of reality by virtue of either ingesting an hallucinogenic substance, or by means of rhythmic sound or movement. While in this state, they have often reported a reality that is far more fluid, dynamic and mutable than the construct that we call our own.

If we think of reality as a broadcast with varying frequencies, depending on the strength of our own internal antenna, we can imagine that the stronger the antenna, the more likely we will be able to experience more channels. In keeping with this metaphor, many alternative theorists believe the reality that is largely accepted is but a *low fidelity* emission that resonates with those who carry a weak signal. Once the antenna is upgraded, the choices for different channels are much easier to attain.

Discovering a reality that is far more preferable to the recipient will require a classic but largely subjective journey, one that is not dictated externally, but is derived internally.

We all have *a priori* knowledge, and yet it seems missing from our structure at present. I don't suppose the discovery of the plasticity of reality will be arrived at collectively, but by each of us being willing to take the wisdom of our ancestors without delay or equivocation, and discover its fluidity for ourselves.

To rationalize a reality that is but a mere construct is to dive toward the mirage before you with an unquenchable thirst anticipating a satisfaction that is *Maya* and has been all along.

It is time we take the journey less traveled and determine truth with all its vibrant colors and hues. In so doing, the dictates of consensus and the pressures to conform to that consensus will indeed melt away like the mirage you approach as you get closer to it. Then you will see, feel and know that you can create the reality that you prefer and *toss* the reality you thought was all there was to experience.

30

"The greatest revolution of our generation is the discovery that human beings, by changing the inner attitudes of their minds, can change the outer aspects of their lives."
-William James

Six

NO REVOLUTION WITHOUT EVOLUTION

Thus far in this collection of essays, we have pointed out that radical change is indeed underway – there is little argument there!

Some are assigning its irrefutable presence to geophysical phenomena (which we will address in detail a little later) – climate change is a reality, solar flares are coming fast and furious, even the gradual reversal of our magnetic poles has gotten airplay in the mainstream.

Others are using prophecy as their measuring stick for the apocalyptic inevitability; Nostradamus, Cayce, cryptic hieroglyphs within the tombs of Egypt – presaging the current times, the Mayans, the Hopi, all have their version of *the now* in which we live.

And still others are immersed in the epidermis layer of our daily reality – economy, global conflict, violence. We are uneasy to be sure.

But how do we respond to such tumult? What is this inevitable shift really beckoning, assuming there is such?

The term "revolution" has seeped its way into pop culture's vocabulary like a video going viral on the Internet. Involved souls have re-ignited their right to use their voice and their actions to "just say no," in a mass choir of occupation and revolt.

Protest has long been mankind's way of cleansing the bloodstream of complacency and acceptance. When we continue to accept status quo, victim mentality will eventually give way to "Wait a minute – what have you been doing to me? No more!" And protest can be a great detoxifier both individually and en masse.

History is filled with accounts of mass revolution giving way to the overthrow of dictatorships and the ushering in of civil rights. No doubt, true democracy in action is participation – which should inevitably lead to the crumbling of a system that's broken, to make way for a new one that works.

But in these unique times for which we live, revolution is only one piece of a greater whole that cannot afford to be overlooked.

Evolution, which is defined as "any process of formation or growth; development," is indeed a part of the revolution process, and as the word implies, the literal meaning will bear out: you cannot have revolution *without* evolution. Stated more clearly, unless the individual is willing to evolve himself – the revolution will be in vain. Thus, we are the change we've been waiting for!

Look at the words and their respective roots:

When you take *revolution*, the root is *revolve*, meaning the act of repeated rotation. This could be taken to mean that one revolves but never goes anywhere – it's just the act of repeating an action or movement.

Evolution yields the verb – *evolve*; the act of growing from seed to flower, from caterpillar to butterfly – a metamorphosis. Simply becoming something that we weren't before.

This is not to say that involving one's self in protest, especially one of peaceful rapport, cannot be effective. History illustrates that this certainly can be. But clearly and honestly, there is an aspect of the human habit that has a hunger to get involved in a cause, just for the sake of taking part. Raising your voice, holding a sign and bonding through that process means something to us. What happens however, is that one can get so wrapped up in the act of protest that they lose sight of what they are protesting about. Then it simply becomes a distraction that allows those we are protesting against to carry on the very thing that we are trying to stop.

Evolution is a natural process of becoming; a gradual union with the All-That-Is. Call it God, Creator – the names are not important, but the unconditional desire to know that state of being and then taking the steps to become closer to it – to evolve, is truly what may be inviting our attention right now.

So what does that mean? Moreover, how do we evolve? The good news is that many individuals are now committed to the process of evolution. Some are opting to make lifestyle changes, whether it is a diet from network news or from the heavily processed foods that we eat. Proliferating acts of kindness and in the spirit of *pay it forward* to spread true and unconditional love throughout the planet, such as we pointed out with the *Bank of Happiness* project are gaining momentum. Periods of quiet and solitude are slowly replacing the "guilty pleasures" of reality TV and thumbing texts at every available moment.

Baby steps toward evolution are leading one up a grander staircase and the result is a shift, not only on our physical planet but in our very consciousness.

Researcher and speaker David Wilcock has a great video presentation whose title speaks volumes. It's called "Occupy Your Self" which you can find on his web site: www.divinecosmos.com. It makes a wonderful and compelling case about the things that we can do both individually and collectively, to bring about the evolutionary shift that is knocking at our door. I urge you to watch it, then sit and contemplate how you might integrate even just a few of these

34

practices into your life for true evolution.

So let's keep in mind as we go about our new found zeal, that unless and until we are willing to embrace and act upon the process of individual evolution, genuine revolution will not and cannot occur. When the collective development of our inner essence burgeons forth, any external revolution will be destined to succeed for the betterment of all mankind.

"The only journey, is the journey within."
-Rainer Maria Rilke

Seven

SPIRITUAL SOVEREIGNTY

Independence is one of those terms that many assign to the position they claim while walking the face of this earth. Are you an independent thinker, worker, or doer? Do you declare yourself independent of any political party? Are you one of those people that simply hate to ask for anything from anyone, because after all, you are fiercely *independent*? What about your *spiritual* independence or sovereignty? Let's weigh in on the importance of the integration of total spiritual freedom into the overall picture of the human personality as we muse about the world in its new state of ever increasing frequency.

~~~

Seeking and finding truth is a sacred and personal endeavor. Truth can be gleaned through a myriad of lenses – interpretations. Getting to the truth of our spiritual selves and the spiritual world from which we spring, an effort earnestly sought by many these days, can be a complex undertaking, especially for those who have not yet claimed their spiritual sovereignty.

From the time we land on this little blue planet, we are exposed and then indoctrinated into some form of belief, be it orthodox or unorthodox. Even non-believers still count their stance (of whatever it is) as "a view" – a precept most probably derived from some external influence or authority (or lack thereof), in their lives. All beliefs then become accepted and adopted; hence they wouldn't be beliefs at all.

The word Gnosis, having Greek origins means *knowledge* or more specifically *spiritual and mystical knowledge.* Practicing Gnostics however didn't just obtain knowledge through external sources or outside authorities. Theirs was a direct interaction with the multidimensional reality to obtain truth. Direct experience thus becomes a knowing. When this is achieved, belief need not apply. It was Einstein who said, "The only source of knowledge is experience."

We are experiential creatures. We are here to explore, to re-connect with our deepest selves, unencumbered. Simply, this is what it means to be spiritual – to breathe freely, purposefully, consciously. Where this fundamental tenet of life is perhaps intellectually endeavored by many, the shackles of external spiritual influence are still refusing to loosen their grip on many a well intentioned human in this process, and as a result, true spiritual sovereignty is usurped.

The modalities and books and courses and workshops that have been placed conveniently in our midst tempt us into believing that these tools will eventually bring us to spiritual enlightenment. Although useful at times, to get to the core of our spiritual selves we must close the book, walk out of the workshop, stop the chanting and just BE.

In Neil Kramer's most excellent volume entitled *The Unfoldment – The Organic Path to Clarity, Power and Transformation* he says, "Doing hours of meditation, following ceremonies and rituals, or even just watching endless online videos, yields little more than mere rumors of illumination. To get to the real thing, it is necessary to first stop everything. Everything. Only by holding still can we go deep beneath the calm of the surface and actually look into the darkness. Whatever is there *is* you. Blemishes, conquests, beauty, mortification, bafflement, and longing – all of it has to be first seen as just what it is."

This articulate recommendation by Kramer tells us that both shadow and light can only be seen and experienced by shutting out the noise; the voices of authority that tell us what spirituality is and how to achieve it. This is Gnosis (knowing), and it engenders a subjective and authentic journey which leads inevitably to enlightenment.

To be that spiritual self; free to grow, unfettered from any external stimuli that may mask itself as an authentic and autonomous steering mechanism to spiritual evolution, is what it means to be spiritually sovereign.

Kramer says, "The sovereign spirit cannot be contracted." Indeed. But to hold our own contract and not outsource it comes responsibility. Not to anyone – but to ourselves. This perhaps is our only purpose here – to be ourselves. At first blush this sounds easy, even unproductive. But with a bit of contemplation it becomes clear that the fact that we live on a planet of such polarity and distinction – pressures to conform to one side or another, this doctrine or that, makes any authentic commitment to being ourselves quite the task, or so it would appear. Therein lies the beauty of the exploration of self. When we realize this very unique set of circumstances for which we are in, the sovereignty of ourselves and achieving that state become all the more grand and accomplished. This makes the journey a truly creative, unbiased, important and personal exploration.

Before closing this piece, allow me one poignant example for the power of spiritual sovereignty or more aptly, a *subjective journey*...

When I was a teen, growing up in an "alternative" household, my parents saw fit to bring me along to a family outing: Transcendental Meditation (TM) class. Yes, I was learning meditation at thirteen along with Mom and Dad. I was handed my mantra, told of course not to tell anyone else what that mantra was, and off I went to practice daily, roughly twenty minutes, along with a substantial list of how-to's that absolutely had to be employed in order for it to be effective. Following the edict of my instructor and the loving encouragement of my parents, I followed directions to the T or TM! The only problem was I was getting nothing out of it! My parents were ardent practitioners of TM, so their story was quite different. Mom swore by its effectiveness and often swapped a two hour nap for a twenty minute power meditation to rejuvenate. Dad even hung a sign on the basement door during his daily practice: "DO NOT DISTURB – TM." I, on the other hand was suspicious of its guaranteed spiritual efficacy, at least for me – until I had the gumption to switch things around a bit. I dropped the mantra, changed my pose and did what felt natural – just *be*. I began to experience my own state of meditative delectation. I was witnessing things and states not told to me during my TM classes. Inherently and intuitively, I knew I had reached my own sense of spiritual sovereignty and this *felt* right.

Now I want to state for the record that TM is a most respectable and often effective form of meditation, practiced and supported by millions. In fact, I give thanks for the opportunity to have been exposed to this modality at such a young age. For this provided impetus for my further exploration, and the realization that spiritual sovereignty is what we are here to personify.

The independent investigation of consciousness makes for an exciting adventure and ignites discovery in all other areas of one's life. Author and researcher Graham Hancock said it best when he stated, "If I am not sovereign over my own consciousness, then I am not sovereign over anything."

Our truth, our journey, ourselves is a sacred script, authored *by* us and *for* us. Let us not miss out on the most exciting part – personal exploration. And each chapter of the script, if written, read and assimilated properly, leads to the same inevitable conclusion – spiritual sovereignty.

Musings of a New World ~ I

Dear Diary:

This morning I woke up and I realized I was dreaming. My whole life I've been "asleep." It took me some time to re-orient myself and get my bearings. When I did, I felt clear headed, lucid, energetic — as if I were just born into a world of fresh insights, unlimited pathways, vivid color, and brilliant light.

I outstretched my arms, took a deep breath, and let out a long exhale of relief as I prepared to face my first day in this new world.

The dream is now behind me and as the moments progress, the scenes are fading from my mind...although I can remember little fragments.

In this dream, I vaguely recall seeing people arguing about who was right and who was wrong, blaming one another for this event or that. I saw scores of people walking stiffly along crowded streets with their heads down and their faces worn. I do remember being angry, resentful, and sad but I can't quite remember what made me this way. I would look out of the window each morning and judge if the weather was "bad" or "good." Then I would head off to work, dreading the day would drag on forever, because I was not doing what I enjoyed. Despite my true aspirations, I knew that it would be impossible to live them out because they told me I had to struggle and work endless hours to make a living if I wanted any chance of having a decent life. I listened. But something was tearing at me from the inside-out. I felt something was awry. But I carried on nonetheless. I'm sure there was more to this dream, but the memory is fading fast...I'm so glad this was just a dream!

As I left my home to depart for what I knew would be an extraordinary day, I greeted people walking, laughing, and motioning "hello." I found myself engaged with others in stimulating discussion about their own dreams (many described them as nightmares) and how they all seemed to have had a similar experience as mine. The collective dream had shifted from one of lack and limitation to abundance and creativity. Everyone was simply giddy over the reality that they were now living in this new world, having new thoughts and living with renewed purpose.

So much to see, do and be — I honestly don't know where to start, but I'm so happy that I was just dreaming this other world and now I can truly know what it means to live free, just as I suspected it was meant to be!

Section Two

The Magic, Mystery & Metaphysics of Potentiality

Whenever I'd hear the words *paranormal* or *supernatural*, it always struck me as odd. The terms seemed somehow to be misnomers; backward and misunderstood descriptions of reality. Though central to the human experience, the paranormal is mostly ignored; tucked away in a little corner or in the closet – never to see the light of day.

American writer and philosopher Elbert Hubbard once said, "The supernatural is the natural, not yet understood."

Where there are some who feel an instinctual pull toward those things that evoke a more mystical quality – sensing that the understanding of the mystery would lead to better understanding themselves, the balance are those who'd rather not look at all – for if they did, the nicely behaved reality they've come to know would be washed away like a perfectly built sandcastle suddenly hit by a tidal wave!

I've always expressed bewilderment over individuals who exert pride over their skepticism about such matters as the paranormal, supernatural and psychic. In fact, I find it rather sad but amusing to see how tenacious people can be about their fiercely defended material reality – thinking somehow that if they were to let their guard down (in effect, open their minds) they would be irrevocably weakened. I never cease to be amazed at how this mindset is so ubiquitous, especially in this day and age!

Perchance, if we were to but look just a little more intently at those *not yet understood* occurrences in our own lives and in the lives of countless people throughout recorded human history, might we be on the road to realizing our innate potential? One of my favorite quotes is from American theoretical physicist and philosopher Richard Feynman who said, "It does not do harm to the mystery to know a little more about it."

In this section, *The Magic, Mystery and Metaphysics of Potentiality*, we will illuminate several phenomena that would be viewed as "paranormal" in scope. Despite a world still based largely on a materialistic system that stubbornly refuses to acknowledge its existence, let alone consider its presence as the fundamental underpinnings of reality, the anecdotes persist in excess!

Life after death, mind over matter, levitation, reincarnation and nonlocal consciousness — these are but some of the anomalies embedded in "material reality" that we will take a brief look at in the following essays.

Moreover, in spite of the persistent appearance of these occurrences in the lives of everyday people, the adamancy of resistance to share these experiences with the very people who have *also* undoubtedly had such phenomena occur in their lives may be costing the species at-large a vital ingredient to their individual and collective evolution.

Will this "new world" continue to tolerate such stubborn naivety? Or will there be a time that in order to live in accord with a highly evolved planet, we must put our own *supernature* to work in order to exist and flourish on this planet?

Let us now contemplate the reality of the magic, mystery, and metaphysics of human potential!

"I would rather live in a world where my life is surrounded by mystery than live in a world so small that my mind could comprehend it."
-Henry Emerson Fosdick

Eight

❧ ❧

THE TRUE NATURE OF REALITY – DO WE REALLY KNOW THE WHOLE STORY?

True Account:

Lisa was grief stricken over the recent loss of her father. She had been talking to her sister on the phone about their dad when all of a sudden the phone went dead. After a second or two of silence, a faint static sound emerged and then a male voice, one that sounded eerily like Lisa's dad said, "Lisa, is that you? Lisa? I'm here, I'm here." The voice then quickly faded away and the conversation with Lisa's sister resumed. Shocked and utterly confused at what clearly appeared to be Lisa's father on the phone AFTER he'd died, mystified both sisters. Could it be that Lisa's dad was still alive, just not in physical form?

~~~

Science continues to grapple with a plethora of unknown and inexplicable events – enigmas such as telepathy, remote viewing, psychokinesis (PK), intuition and even the possibility of the survival of consciousness after physical death. Some scientists are now slowly relenting to the possibility that there may indeed be more to the "sticks and stones" rigidity of our physical Universe than what has heretofore been described.

From a more spiritually based perspective, a number of books which reflect the public's desire to validate unexplained personal experience have cropped up in record numbers within recent years. Titles such as *The Celestine Prophecy*, *Conversations with God*, *The Seat of the Soul*, and *Talking to Heaven* initiated a launch into the inquiry of the unknown, garnering prestigious best selling status and setting the template for what would become a burgeoning new interest, simply because – *people want answers.*

Mainstream television is now even attempting to satisfy the rising curiosity of the public's desire to know more about the *unknown* with shows about psychic children, ghostly encounters with celebrities and UFO abductions. But despite the increasing presence of these programs, the unanswered questions still persist and unfortunately for many, the "giggle factor" of such topics does as well!

Regardless of how it is presented, the very incidence of phenomena in our everyday world is more of a reflection of our true nature and process, than the picture of reality that we've all been taught in our high school science class.

No doubt, there is a growing curiosity about these phenomena. But still, many people are oblivious to the fact that for years, a scrupulous and scholarly pursuit has been underway in order to try and comprehend the dynamics of metaphysics, the paranormal and the true nature of reality.

Though some will at least utilize its mystical thought provoking elements for periodic after dinner discussion, despite the empirical evidence of our historical record, the subject matter is considered nothing more than novelty at best, appropriate only for frivolous and social interest.

This essay is written as an attempt to veer us away from the novelty motivation of the subject matter and get us to take an important look at the potential life changing implications of the subject matter. For if this is the *stuff* from and for which we are made, by paying closer attention and honing our intrinsic abilities while embracing the mystery, we may change our life in profound and positive ways.

In one of his last interviews, the late author, Michael

Talbot said, when being asked why he is interested in such "weird" things he responded, "...it's not that I'm just interested in the 'weird,' I am interested in what these things have to teach us and the practical applications."

In the introduction to their book *Miracles of Mind*, renowned physicist and ESP researcher, Russell Targ and spiritual healer, Dr. Jane Katra convey, "Our psychic and spiritual capacities enable us to explore an important part of our true nature. Accepting and learning to use our non-local minds is important because it gives us direct access to the wider world in which we reside. It shows us that our consciousness knows no boundaries. We can each personally contact this expansive dimension of life, which evokes in us a greater sense of what our purpose here might be, and inspires us to reach for our highest potential as conscious beings."

The paradox is frustrating and perplexing and is simply this – Since time immemorial, humans have been vitally interested in the questions about the self and its place in the Universe; who we are, what we represent, and our purpose. And yet most people will avoid the reality of phenomena, for fear it may open up Pandora's Box. Invariably, the issue gets obliterated from awareness, due to the everyday focus of action and reaction on the surface of existence. We become so passionately focused in the world of appearances and circumstances, that we simply forget to step back and take the time to contemplate the possible causation for those very appearances and circumstances.

Targ says, "...as a scientist I aim to demonstrate that we significantly misunderstand our inter-connectedness, and our place in the space-time matrix in which we appear to be embedded." Suffice it to say, reality is much bigger than we can currently comprehend. We are simply focused on only a tiny fraction of it. The misunderstanding of the scope, or lack thereof, of reality and moreover our connection to it, may be costing us greatly!

After speaking with a significant number of individuals on a variety of personal experiences which would be categorized as "paranormal," and their general feeling about the validity of these experiences, my surmise is that many, if not most people suspect that there is more to reality than what we have been taught in formal settings.

Even those who are considered the most ardent of skeptics, if prodded enough, would probably admit to having an experience or two that does not fit within the "normal" and familiar constructs of reality as we know it. Their mission is to come up with an explanation that would wipe the experience off the board of possibility. Unless the experience can be presented with some justification like, "I was just overly tired," or "it was just a coincidence," it cannot and should not be looked at again. This is just an example of course, as to how the human mind is so conditioned to ignore phenomena that has not as yet been objectively or scientifically supported.

I find it rather ironic that Sir Isaac Newton, who some consider to be the father of classical physics, was himself a mystic. Newton was born in the mid 1600's, a time when astrology and astronomy went hand-in-hand and alchemical practices were more readily known. Still, Newton's on-the-record discoveries forged a path toward a more materialistic view of reality, consigning the mystical to fantasy and self deception. Newton was an alchemist himself and it is said that his knowledge of the paranormal greatly influenced his discoveries!

Here we are now in the twenty-first century, living according to an agreed-upon belief system, most of which obey the laws of physics quite nicely. Regardless of the possible cultural, religious and academic delineation, it is only when you abstract the individual out of the conventional consensus environment that they will give in and share experiences which don't necessarily follow the everyday construct that has been put before them by society.

Interestingly, it is among these same individuals who have experienced phenomena on a broad and diverse scale and often on a regular basis, who are part and parcel of the consensus building to begin with – and yet, they will unequivocally and passionately convey the realness of their own experience but deem the experience as irrelevant to "everyday reality," thereby making it unimportant.

Although these incidents, whereby anecdotal in nature may tell them otherwise, the tendency is to cling to the familiar picture they know and are comfortable with. Perhaps it is out of a fear of societal ridicule that people tend to hang onto the fundamental core reasoning of reality rather than letting experience be their guide. On the other-hand, ridicule may only be a partial explanation for this vehement denial. Whatever the cause, it must be contemplated that to deny the true nature of reality is to deny the true nature of *self.*

In their 1995 book, *Hello from Heaven* by Bill and Judy Guggenheim, they document hundreds of personal experiences of those who have had what they refer to as an after-death communication or ADC; a direct communication from an individual who has passed away. Among the various ways that ADC's can happen, "telephone ADC's" – hearing the voice of the deceased over the phone, is somewhat uncommon, but they do occur. Similar to the case of Lisa who heard her deceased father during a phone call with her sister, telephone ADC's are one of the more perplexing of after-death phenomena.

Although rare, this form of ADC is only one of a number of other means the departed use to contact us. Two more accounts well worth sharing before we close this essay, involve the touching stories of Cissy Houston, mother of the late pop star Whitney Houston and jazz legend Nancy Wilson – my own "mom" whom I affectionately call "Mom Suzy."

It was on Saturday, February 11, 2012 when the world received shocking news of the sudden death of Whitney Houston after apparently drowning in the bath tub of her hotel suite in Beverly Hills, California. Earlier in the afternoon, Whitney's mom Cissy was in her apartment 3,000 miles away on the east coast when all of a sudden, she heard her doorbell ring. She hadn't been expecting anyone. Curious, she walked to the door and opened it, but no one was there. Moments later, the bell rang again – no one there! Now clearly irritated, she then called the building's front desk to ask whether anyone had come to see her. "No Mrs. Houston," the concierge replied. It was not long after the mysterious doorbell episode that Cissy received the news of Whitney's death!

The previous Christmas, Whitney, who close friends and family members called *Nippy*, had spent some time with Cissy, and just prior to her leaving to go back to her home in Atlanta, she promised emphatically that she would come back to see her mother, after the Grammy awards in Los Angeles in February. Of course that was not to happen…or did Whitney actually keep her promise after all, despite her untimely passing? After the inconceivable reality of her daughter's death sunk in, Cissy says that she took comfort in one thing – "On that terrible day, when my doorbell kept ringing in those hours before [I got the] call, I believe it was my beautiful Nippy, keeping her promise to me – that somehow, some way, she came to see me, just as she said she would."

ADC's can come in a number of ways and at the most unexpected times, although many report that the after-death communication often happens during a time when comfort and reassurance are needed.

My cousin, whom I call *Mom Suzy* is known to the rest of the world for her incredible ability to seamlessly weave detailed narration into her chart-topping hits. Known by many as "the Song-stylist," Grammy award winning jazz artist, Nancy Wilson tells colorful stories through her music, but she also has a natural ability to recall stories about all sorts of things, remembering details about our family, holiday gatherings from years past, even exact quotes of what "Aunt Jenny said about...this or that." But it was this story that she told me shortly after her husband of over thirty years, Wiley Burton passed away after a lengthy illness...

"I was in the house alone and it was one of those rare occasions when we were getting snow up here." Her home sits roughly 3,500 feet above the desert area of Palm Springs, California. "I was in my bedroom and a little concerned about the snow and the fact that it might be difficult to navigate the cars without the drive being plowed. All of a sudden, I heard Wiley's voice: 'Nancy, are you alright?' I got up out of bed and walked toward the room where he'd spent his last days, bedridden. I knew damn well that he was gone. Why would I walk to that room? But his voice was clear. It was unmistakable. I still can't explain it."

When she first told me this story, I smiled and nodded my head, remembering how Wiley always found it so exciting that snow would occasionally fall on his beloved Pipes Canyon Ranch. He'd always get all worked up like it was such a big deal!

After death communications happens to people from all

walks of life, and have been occurring probably since the beginning of time. Some have absolutely no doubt of the authenticity of the experience, while others question its validity altogether.

When Lisa conveyed the story to me about her deceased father coming through on the phone, although momentarily suspended with passion about the actuality of the experience, she then shrugged her shoulders and said, "oh well, I don't *really* believe in these sorts of things…" Clearly, her denial spoke volumes to what she had accepted as reality. Her long held beliefs would always take precedence over her personal experience – no matter what!

When experience becomes our sole compass for reality, its true nature will reveal itself to us in ways that are limitless, and in the process we will recognize that we too are limitless in our abilities. Our beliefs will then take a back-seat to that which is undeniable in the spectrum of an infinite reality. The time has come for us to know *the whole story*.

"Reality is merely an illusion, albeit a very persistent one."
-Albert Einstein

Nine

❧ ❦

TRANSCENDING THE RULES OF REALITY

To the mainstream, physical reality denotes the fixed variables for which we live. Circumstances and events are created out of cause and effect, and for this reality is largely deterministic. If you cut yourself – you bleed, if you touch a hot stove – you'll be burned, etc.

But what if we are only experiencing part of what reality has to offer and moreover, what if the rules of reality can be bent?

There are some fascinating examples, which suggest that reality may indeed be plastic and that the rules by which most of us have come to abide, are not etched in stone.

Although the general picture of reality and the laws set forth notably by Sir Isaac Newton's mechanistic universal model still represent the building blocks of our understanding thus far, cutting edge research and the study of reality within the context of quantum theory may yield a different picture entirely. That picture of the mysterious workings and interactions of the Universe and our function within it, are slowly making its way to the forefront.

Most of us look to science to determine and thus define the rules of reality, but there are many an impressive and credible case of those seemingly inexplicable events which intimate a reality far more vast and fluid than most people realize.

We have all heard incredible stories of individuals who were considered "special" in that they were able to transcend reality and as a result, perform feats and overcome obstacles that seem to violate the very rules that reality has shown us.

One startling and well-known example is that of a young girl who lived in the mid to late nineteenth century in Lourdes, France named Bernadette Soubirous. Her incredible devotion to the Virgin Mary and the mysterious apparitions of her, which made Lourdes a shrine for religious devotees, was the site where little Bernadette would go into meditation. On one occasion, the municipal physician of Lourdes who had witnessed the ritualistic process of Bernadette in meditation decided to make note of her actions. Bernadette, he noticed, had lowered her hand into the flame of a candle during meditation, and remained in that position for nearly ten minutes. Once she came out of her meditative trance, he noticed that the flame of the candle did not burn, scorch, or harm her flesh in any way!

Fire immunity – the ability to overcome any physical effects of fire and extreme heat, is something that clearly defies the laws of physics and yet there have been many well-documented cases of such feats. The Hawaiian Kahunas practice the ritual of "invoking the gods," reciting lengthy prayers to protect them and then walking over hot lava while emerging from the practice unscathed.

In Vincent Gaddis' 1967 book, *Mysterious Fires and Lights* he documents the story of a New York physician who encountered a twelve year old boy while on a hunting trip in the Tennessee mountains. The young boy had the ability to handle red-hot irons while being impervious to its effects. He told the physician that he had discovered this ability when he accidentally picked up a red-hot horseshoe in his uncle's blacksmith shop.

As astonishing as the implications of fire immunity appear

to be, there are yet other equally "miraculous" stories which have been inked in the history of reality transcending phenomena.

One such example appears in Dr. Bernie Siegel's book, *Love, Medicine and Miracles*, in which a terminal cancer patient given only a short time to live learns of a new experimental cancer drug called *Krebiozen*. Although the patient's diagnosis was grim and his survival seemingly hopeless, he begged his physician to give him the drug in a last ditch effort to save him. The doctor although reluctant, finally gave in and treated the patient with the new drug. Miraculously, over a relatively short period of time, the doctor reported that the patient's "orange sized" tumors had "melted like snowballs on a hot stove!" The patient regained strength and was subsequently sent home nearly cancer free.

Clearly confounded, the physician hastened to find an explanation to his patient's miraculous recovery.

It wasn't until a medical journal report came out about the drug which seemed to indicate that the drug's effects were not as positive as first thought. The patient read these reports and became depressed. After being checked back into the hospital, the physician found that his tumors had re-appeared and his condition quickly worsened. It was at this time that the doctor realized that what was having the *real* effect on his patient was not the drug, but rather his *faith* in the drug. Acting like a placebo, the news of the drug placed a powerful suggestion within the patient, and a subsequent healing ensued. Now the suggestion was reversed, and the illness cropped back up.

Feeling that this was indeed what was occurring, the physician decided to tell his patient that the reports that were published were wrong and that there was an even better version of the drug and that he would administer it to his patient. He then injected the patient with nothing but fresh water. The result? Again, tumors melted like snowballs on a hot stove and the man was again sent home.

Unfortunately, the final report of the drug Krebiozen was published and found unequivocally to be of no use in treating cancer. The patient again read the reports, relapsed into illness and died shortly thereafter.

On its own, this is a poignant account; one that raises an eyebrow as to the actual process of reality creation and transcendence. The idea of a placebo having a distinct effect on a patient is not new. This has been studied for some time and at great length. But what may *actually* be occurring has yet to be studied in the exhaustive manner that it deserves.

The burning question becomes what is the actual catalyst in transcending the rules of reality? What agent makes this so? In all of the above cases, the answer seems obvious: *faith and belief*.

Simply put, maybe faith can do more than move mountains (although this would be quite an achievement), but also render a person harmless from extreme heat and cure illness, in addition to a myriad of other possibilities.

Are these but notable anecdotal miracles allocated to "special" persons, or is the mere knowledge of such experience meant to enlighten us to our own reality transcending abilities that currently lie dormant within the consciousness of man?

If these and hundreds of other similar stories are intimating that consciousness can manipulate the seemed rigid framework of reality, then why do most of us experience a fixed reality, nicely obeying the laws of physics?

The answer quite frankly, may be the same as to how some individuals can change reality: faith and belief. One of the most fundamental of human characteristics is habit. We are simply habitual creatures. So too are our thoughts and beliefs a result of habitual thinking. Even more so is the notion that most of our thoughts and beliefs are beneath conscious awareness and therefore not easily accessible for change. It is only when we attempt to swim beneath the surface of conscious awareness and tap the unconscious thoughts that guide us through life that we may experience a change in our own reality.

It is a fascinating prospect. Imagine what we might achieve if we commit to searching our memory banks for those thoughts and beliefs that have largely shaped our reality, discard the ones that no longer serve us, and adopt new beliefs that do. Obviously we are not speaking of becoming impervious to fire per se, but if reality is indeed a construct waiting for new rules to adhere to and we ultimately make those rules, of course the possibilities for transformation become an infinite spectrum.

Through conviction alone we may be able to tap the well-spring of the Universe, in order to show us a much broader picture of reality. A picture better suited to our spiritual needs and overall well being. What an encouraging notion!

"We would do much better to embrace the magic than to turn our back on its bequest."
-The Author

Ten

❧ ❧

GEOPHYSICAL PHENOMENA
& THE THINNING VEIL

Leo Deis, a 76 year old man from Regina, Canada nearly had his paradigm shattered when he witnessed firsthand, a broom in his family home stand on its own. The bristled broomstick, suspended with no aid whatsoever, remained in an upright position on their tiled floor for a significant amount of time. Deis was not the only one in his family to witness this apparent feat of wizardry. Inquisitive, he decided to take a paintbrush to the floor to see if it would obey these new laws of physics he had recently discovered. To his amazement, the brush followed suit and remained suspended as well with no support at all.

Apparently, the phenomenon of unsupported brooms has been sweeping across the planet and reported by store owners, housewives and news media alike. So, what is going on?

Deis was quick to point out his interest and previous study of physics and chemistry, and reasoned that this anomalous act might be an epiphenomenon from the recent high solar activity that had been taking place.

It is certainly difficult to ignore the fact that a variety of strange and unusual phenomena have been occurring in recent years, although some date these increased effects back to the 1800's.

The Geophysical Factor

Is there indeed some correlation between these phenomena and erratic geophysical activity (GPA)?

When I spoke with author and paranormal researcher Rosemary Ellen Guiley to get her take on whether GPA might account for an increase in reported paranormal activity, here's what she had to say...

"Many people have speculated that activity in the earth's magnetic field has bearing on this and I do believe that to be the case. We have cycles and solar activity where increased solar flares activate the magnetosphere and paranormal investigations indicate that spirit communications and even the manifestations of entities seem to be sensitive to fluctuations in the magnetic energy. There are places on the earth for example that have dramatic negative magnetic anomalies and these almost always are associated with intense hot zones and paranormal activity on an ongoing basis."

Although science is quick to point out that there is no hard evidence to support these claims, they do admit that the sun's magnetic field is "flipping," and that solar maximum is here.

In an article posted on the NASA Science News web site in 2001, scientists state, "The sun's magnetic poles will remain as they are now, with the north magnetic pole pointing through the sun's southern hemisphere, until the year 2012 when they will reverse again. This transition happens, as far as we know, at the peak of every 11-year sunspot cycle, like clockwork."

However, there seem to be additional significant elements that combined with the sun's erratic behavior, are making for an abnormal intersection of activity; the effects of which we haven't seen for perhaps thousands of years.

It is well documented that the earth's magnetic field is

weakening, a feature that gradually but inevitably precedes a full-on pole shift. Many scientists agree that pole reversal has occurred many times over the millennia, and yet most are hard-pressed to admit that we will experience a total pole shift in our lifetime. Others disagree. Author and speaker Gregg Braden is among those doing research in this field who believes that we are in the midst of a shift on many levels. In his landmark book *Awakening to Zero Point*, he describes something he calls the *Shift of the Ages*; a time in earth's history and in human consciousness when a "convergence of decreasing planetary magnetic and increasing planetary frequency upon a point in time" takes place. "The shift represents a rare opportunity of collectively repatterning the expression of human consciousness."

This *repatterning* may very well be resulting in changes to the human sensory system, and experienced both physiologically and psychologically.

Many are reporting irregular patterns of sleep, often waking during the hours between 2am-4am. Additionally, there have been many who I have personally spoken to who have insisted that they have been awakened by either a non-physical being of some sort (some have called them "shadow-like" beings) or even balls of light floating around the room, of which the experiencer *senses* some form of intelligence. Of course there have been many variations to these reports.

Others tell of extremely vivid, sometimes precognitive dreams. Telepathy seems to be on the increase. The act of manifesting based on thought alone is not a new concept, although we are hearing many more cases of instant manifestation in our daily lives.

Lynne McTaggart points out in her book, *The Intention Experiment* how geomagnetic fluctuations in earth's atmosphere can have a significant impact on the consciousness of an individual. Especially during periods of moderate to high solar activity, the act of sending conscious intention seems to be far more effective. Interestingly though, when solar activity is low, thereby resulting in quiet to no geomagnetic "storminess," the faculty known as psi whereby the individual is more tuned to receiving information is greater.

My surmise is that both sending and receiving of psychic information has reached a crescendo – due perhaps in part to the heightened geophysical phenomena we are experiencing on a regular basis.

Our psychic faculties and the interpenetration of our awareness into these realms are but one, albeit important feature of this "new energy" we are experiencing. Braden points out however, "...it is the awareness of humankind, and not the life essence itself, that is used to interpret the three dimensional world...It is this awareness that is locked up within the fields of magnetics surrounding our planet. Through the structure provided as fields of magnetics the net of our awareness matrix is stabilized and secured in place."

However, now with the steady *decrease* of magnetic shielding, the persistent *increase* of earth frequency along with the fury of solar activity, a potpourri of possibilities are being hurled our way.

What does one do with all of this?

I've no doubt that the complexities of just what is going on here, leaving hints as they may, are more than most can get their heads around – science included! But as is often noted, nature leaves clues if one is attuned to its subtle information.

If we can just imagine that earth has a consciousness and a

body, and "heartbeat" just as we do, we can also reason that resonance between these two bodies (of man and earth) is a natural phenomenon. When the predominant energy changes, the other must follow in like manner – this is the physical law of resonance.

When the earth's protective shield weakens or diminishes, we might liken that to our own protective shield or barrier or veil weakening as well – that of conscious perception. When the veil thins we, just as the earth, have access to all the other information "out there." This flow pours in like a monsoon, but if one is not ready or is unprepared, this evolution will mask itself and be interpreted as tumult, discord and confusion, thus a misunderstanding of the significance of this convergence of energies.

When one consciously recognizes and tunes one's self to the increased frequency of earth's vibration, the veils of perception, polarity, and dissonance begin to dim and the recognition of being one with an unbroken whole starts to emerge. Though beginning individually, a collective awakening starts to take shape.

Braden says, "It is no longer necessary to go into the sacred chambers of ancient structures designed to provide the appropriate environment for this Shift; we are living The Shift within our offices, schools, living rooms as day-to-day life."

So as we ponder the broom anomaly or stretch to make sense of our own fantastical and non-ordinary experiences, let us remind ourselves that we are living during a most unprecedented and magical time; a time that brings forth an opportunity to truly merge with the Shift of the Ages. Let us embrace the magic, attune to its frequency and reap the unlimited benefits of an infinite spectrum of experience.

"…*if a spiritual world exists, and if that world has at any epoch been manifest or even discoverable, then it ought to be manifest or discoverable now.*"

-*F.W.H. Myers*

Eleven

IS PARANORMAL THE NEW NORMAL?

Now that we have a working theoretical framework which might explain the increased anomalies we are experiencing, namely an alteration of the geophysical constituents that make up our planet, let's look at the prospect of what we call "paranormal" as becoming an integrative component for the world in which we reside. We begin with a personal account that in her terms, "defied logic."

~~~

One Sunday in late December of 2012, I had been quietly relaxing at home when all of a sudden an urgent message came via text. "Call me now!", thumbed a friend. She had also left a message both on my cell phone and home line. I knew something was clearly wrong.

I was finally able to reach her, bracing for some horrible news when she said, "Are you sitting down? I can't – I *can't* believe what just happened...I had to call you because you'd be the only one who would understand." "Understand what?" I asked, eagerly awaiting some unbelievable drama that had just unfolded. She then explained in as calm a voice as she could muster, how she was alone at home, washing dishes. She had placed a freshly dried pot and lid on the counter at the other end of the kitchen (and she has a long kitchen), when all of a sudden the lid lifted off of the pot and literally spiraled like a fast moving disc in mid air, landing right at the tip of her left foot, twenty or so feet away from where it rested dormant.

When she was able to finally gather herself enough to make sure she fit all the details of the bizarre encounter in, I was sure to encourage her to go through all possible *logical* explanations as to how this could have happened. "Are you sure it didn't just fall to the ground? Was there any moisture on the pot that might have made it slide out of position, et al?" She stuck exactly to her story. Once we were both clear *something* out of the ordinary was going on, our conversation took on a more, shall we say – *paranormal tone*. She confessed that shortly after the incident occurred, she thought it might have been her aunt who had died only months earlier, making an unexpected visit. "Was that you Auntie? What do you want?"

Offering my usual pragmatic but open minded approach, I asked her why she thought it was her deceased aunt. She then explained that only two days prior to the incident, her husband had just cleared the last of her aunt's belongings from her home and brought many items back to their house, stored in the living room. She went on to say that most of the items were family heirlooms and antiques, some going back several generations. We counted that as one possibility for the paranormal activity; that perhaps the energy emanating from some of the items, allowed for a residual memory to cause a sort of poltergeist phenomenon. Additionally, I asked her about her state of mind at the time of the incident, fishing for some possible explanation of self-induced poltergeist activity that may have been triggered by an intense emotional state. She conceded that she had been thinking about something that roused a sense of anger and frustration in her.

The bottom line is that whether the impetus for this incident was caused by the ghostly remnants of her aunt or her own emotional state, the experience was real and yet unaccounted for.

Of course, similar incidents have maintained a constant throughout recorded human history. And yet, for some reason, more of these types of incidents are being reported in recent years. Many argue that it isn't that paranormal activity has increased per se, but the means of communicating these sorts of things has increased, especially since the advent of the Internet.

In my previous discussion with Rosemary Ellen Guiley she stated, "The media attention on the paranormal and spiritual realms stimulates more people to talk about their own experiences. We do have a factor of increased reporting – not necessarily an increase in actual cases. But because there's no baseline, we have no idea of knowing exactly where that starts and stops. However, I do believe that things are on the increase."

I tend to concur. As you will recall, in my conversation with Rosemary, we also touched upon the unprecedented shift in our geomagnetic field, perhaps generated by the increased solar activity including solar flares and coronal mass ejections – all lighting up the magnetosphere and possibly triggering a pattern of energetic interference of all kinds. Bottom line, the environment for paranormal activity is primed to manifest!

Anecdotal evidence for such things seems to be bearing this out, and scientific corroboration may not be too far behind.

Where certainly our propensity to witness such encounters has never been considered *normal*, perhaps we have just arrived at the threshold of the *new normal*.

About three or so weeks after my friend's paranormal admission, my husband and I had a curious encounter of our own that would add credence to this new reality…

71

Interestingly, we were relaxing in the same room in which I had been conversing with my friend about her own hair raising experience. My husband had just finished a small cup of soup which he was sipping from a modest glass coffee cup. Once finished, he gently placed the cup on the table in front of him and within seconds, the cup literally combusted into what seemed to be a million pieces, sprawled all over the floor and couch! Again, with our normal logical deduction we wondered, "Was the cup still very hot? Did he somehow fracture it when placing it on the table, etc?" Once we were able to rule out all measure of physical cause to the best of our ability, we determined *something* strange was going on. The cup did not crack, it spontaneously combusted directly in front of us. Thank goodness, none of the shards injured either of us!

We must consider the possibility that what we were accustomed to as standard reality, is morphing into an altogether different one, forcing us to redefine our explanation of reality – a world that no longer plays by the same rules that we once knew.

It is my feeling that if we maintain a keen sense of awareness of these things, these formerly *paranormal* occurrences will become ever more prevalent in our lives, and lead us to realizing that our own potential and abilities will be anything *but* normal within the reality for which we now reside.

Welcome to the *New Normal!*

"...I am confident in the belief that there truly is such a thing as living again, and that the living spring from the dead, and that the souls of the dead are in existence..."
-Socrates

Twelve

❧ ❧

BIRTH-MARKING PAST LIVES

When we think of the word "normal," several images come to mind. We are born, nurtured by our family, sent off to live, work and exist in the world that is now so familiar to us. Our expectations are, well, *normal* – at least for most people. But every once in a while we find ourselves right smack in the middle of a mind-twisting mystery. "Why is my child constantly talking about being a soldier in WWII and *why* does he know so much about my great grandfather? How could he possibly have gotten this information?" Enter the phenomenon of past lives. Do they exist? Are they common? Are we, now in this physical form just one of perhaps hundreds of previous personalities that have walked the face of this earth? Let's continue to explore the mysteries of *life and potentiality* through the eyes of the past.

~~~

The grandmother of a little boy from Thailand made a fervent request while she lay dying: "When I come back, I want to be a male." When the woman eventually passed away, her daughter-in-law took some white paste and drew a broad line on the back of the deceased woman's neck, in hopes that one day she would be identified in her next life.

The little boy, named Cloy, was born just a few years after his grandmother's passing. Clearly noticeable at his birth was a white line on the back of his neck, as if someone had drawn it directly onto his skin.

As he got older and could communicate, he began to state emphatically that he *is* his grandmother! His adamancy grew, even to the point where he exclaimed that the rice field which his grandmother once owned belonged to him!

In some Asian countries, there is a common practice that involves marking the deceased with ash or paste so that when the soul is reincarnated, the relatives can recognize them from the designated marking.

Although markings (birthmarks) or even deformities of the body are less documented among the cases of past life evidence, they do occur. The details are still quite nebulous as to where birthmarks originate from, although roughly eighty percent of all babies are born with some sort of mark or discoloration on their body. Sometimes the marks fade over the years and other times they remain.

In my essay, *The Phenomenon of Animal Reincarnation*, which you will read following this piece, I drew from my own personal encounter with what I suspect to be the rebirth of my beloved Persian cat "Paws" (now "Clover Paws"). Uncannily, the new kitten displayed the same identical birth mark as my former cat. Both eventually faded over time. This encounter has inspired me to explore further into one of the more profound clues as to the validity of reincarnation.

The late Dr. Ian Stevenson, a pioneer in parapsychology research and particularly the study of the past lives of children, authored a seminal work which was published in 1993 in an academic journal entitled *Birthmarks and Birth Defects Corresponding to Wounds on Deceased Persons*. In it he stated, "Among 895 cases of children who claimed to remember a previous life (or were thought by adults to have had a previous life), birthmarks and/or birth defects attributed to the previous life were reported in 309 (35%) of the subjects. The birthmark or birth defect of the child was said to correspond to a wound (usually fatal) or other mark on the deceased person whose life the child said it remembered."

Although the aforementioned case of the little boy Cloy whose mark seemed to emanate from his previous life as his grandmother was not the result of a violent infliction of some kind, it still leaves clues as to how the physical remnants of a former incarnation can carry over into the next life.

Still, according to past life research, it appears that many of the documented cases of reincarnation yielding physical marks or scars, corresponded with a violent or traumatic account of the reincarnated individual which most often led to his or her death.

Dr. Jim Tucker, medical director of the Child and Family Psychiatry Clinic and Associate Professor of Psychiatry and Neurobehavioral Medicine at the University of Virginia's School of Medicine, who wrote the book *Life Before Life – Children's Memories of Previous Lives* along with Dr. Stevenson said, "Certainly, I think birthmarks and birth defects argue that there is something that has carried that trauma with it to another life and affected the fetus." Tucker's data indicates that physical trauma in one life can carry over.

Out of 2,500 cases that Tucker studied, roughly 2,000 of them involved cases of traumatic death. For some reason, the mind seems to have the ability to record and vividly recall past trauma and inflict it on the new body. In a strange but not so uncommon correlation, I have read of cases of individuals who encountered violent episodes in their dream states – only to wake up with wounds, scratches, and even blood stains that corresponded to the violence encountered in the dream.

In some way, what is intimated here is that the consciousness of the individual has the ability to manifest (or be a conduit for) a physical marking, be it from a previous life or a violent scuffle in the dreamscape!

Can we remember a previous life from our birthmark?

This is a curious phenomenon – that of the origin of birthmarks. Would it be possible to somehow use our birthmarks as a reference to a possible remembrance of a past life?

Before we rush to answer this question, let us assume that many if not most birthmarks are simply minor defects of the skin during the forming and development of the fetus or even a result from the birthing process itself. But if you felt somehow more drawn to, or simply inquisitive about a particular birthmark you have, you might consider a process called *divination* – in which you use various forms of perceptual tools like intuition to glean significance based on a given object or situation. You might take a photo (or have someone take a photo for you) of the particular mark, print it out, and simply meditate on it, recording the visual of the mark in your mind and recall it during meditation. Similarly, you might focus on the image of the mark just prior to falling asleep, and request a dream that might leave some clues as to its origin. Or you could see one of many good past life regression therapists who might suggest working with your birthmark as a focus for hypnosis. There are quite a few creative options to investigate.

One caution however – before you embark on such an adventure like discovering a past life, be certain that you *want* to know about the life you previously led. Inquiry just for curiosity's sake, can often prove to be less desirable than you might have expected. Obviously make your decision to explore this other life of yours with total responsibility. On the other hand, if you choose to go forward, you may discover a pertinent clue as to who and what you are today and how to *be* a better you! Nonetheless, this is certainly a fascinating subject to explore.

Tucker says, "The explanation for how this carry-over [memory] occurs, largely remains to be elucidated, but in general terms, the ideas that consciousness is not purely a creation of the brain; consciousness can be considered a separate entity *from* the physical brain and continue on in another life."

The mysteries of the Universe and of ourselves continue…

"Until one has loved an animal, a part of one's soul remains unawakened."
-Anatole France

Thirteen

❧ ❧

THE PHENOMENON OF ANIMAL REINCARNATION – THEIR POTENTIAL THROUGH OUR EYES

"The Universe is quite marvelous!" That's what past life regression expert, Dr. Bruce Goldberg, responded with when I relayed to him the following story…

It was mid October of 2012, when I had been casually perusing a cat breeder's web site – something I would occasionally do as I inched closer to the idea of getting a new kitty after our beloved Persian, "Paws," passed away the previous February. On this particular visit to the site, I noticed an offering I had not seen before: an eight month old male, doll faced, copper eyed white Persian named "Clover" who had been available for months. I could hardly believe my eyes (or his) – he looked *identical* to my Paws. I had been to the breeder's site several times before. Why hadn't I noticed him?

After showing my husband Clover's picture, his astonishment at first glance matched mine. We'd looked at perhaps hundreds of pictures of white Persian kittens with the same general attributes, but no kitten looked so much like our departed pet. In no time, we were on the phone to the breeder to ask a few pertinent questions. Could this be our new – or *re-newed* kitty? It was then that she conveyed some facts about this kitten that nearly knocked me out of my seat!

Clover had been born with a little gray birthmark on the top of his head that has slowly faded as he's gotten older. Paws had the same mark in the same spot, slowly fading at about nine months! Clearly, there are some breeds of white Persians that do have this characteristic, but I had never seen any kittens with this feature since Paws'. She then said that he was the only male in his litter...so was Paws! And then the kicker: Clover was born merely *hours* within the time that Paws passed, taking his last breath in the arms of a loving caretaker, while I was on assignment, 3,000 miles away in California to interview, none other than Dr. Goldberg, about the subject of conscious dying and past lives!

At this point, the similarities to me and to my husband had far surpassed the notion of chance! Could the soul of my precious Paws have jumped from his frail little body into a brand new one, just waiting for us to find him? Adding to the curious circumstances surrounding this eight month old kitten – the breeder conveyed to me how perplexed she was as to why *no one* had even inquired about this adorable little fur ball! In all the kittens she'd sold, this had never happened before! It was pretty clear to me what was going on!

Animal reincarnation is a subject that has been discussed within the larger subject of past lives and has increased in interest in recent years. Due in part to the growing trend of animal companionship as a central part of the modern lifestyle, pets have increasingly taken center stage in millions of people's lives. In a 2009 Time magazine article, statistics showed that in the last fifteen years, spending on our much-loved pets has grown from $17 billion to $43 billion annually! Pet bereavement groups have popped up in record number – an unknown phenomenon not so long ago. In fact, I documented in my initial interview with Dr. Goldberg, the story of a woman who had recently lost her dog and fell into a clinical depression. Goldberg used a technique in which he guided the woman into an altered state he calls "In the Body Experience" or IBE – somewhat similar to an OBE, except the consciousness is still grounded within the physical form during the experience. The woman claimed emphatically that she met her lost pet while in the IBE state. They shared a profound reunion which paved the way for a complete healing of her depression.

Not long after this extraordinary experience, the woman found another dog, inexplicably sitting in her parked car upon return from a shopping trip. She brought the dog home and noticed striking similarities in personality to her "deceased" pet! To this day, she is absolutely sure that this animal is her former pet, reincarnated!

Although we don't fully understand how reincarnation works, the re-entrance of the soul into physical form seems to be a consistent part of the framework of reality and one that has been documented throughout history. Why would animals be precluded from this process?

When Clover finally arrived at our home in November of 2012, the last thing I wanted to do was to set myself up for disappointment, thinking that he was a reincarnated Paws. After all, we didn't get this little kitten because we thought this was Paws, but because it just seemed natural to have him. Besides, it wouldn't be wise to expect the same cat to walk through the doors he was carried out of nine months ago, never to return. But much to my surprise, when Clover arrived, save for a period of a few hours of anxiety over his long connecting flight from Kansas City to Houston to Boston, he settled right in to our home. The next day, I keenly observed what to him seemed like *familiar surroundings*. He proceeded to Paws' favorite dining room chair, and lounging atop the mahogany table (a habit that I steadily tried to break in

Paws, but to no avail). He follows me everywhere, giving me that same wide eyed "play with me" look. There are other similarities between both cats, too numerous to mention. Not just a few characteristics, but virtually *everything* that Paws famously exhibited, Clover was doing and quickly! My expectation of clear differences between the two was quickly eclipsed by what seemed to be the exact same kitty! He was just picking up where he left off nine months previous!

The phenomenon of reincarnation is an elusive subject among many, that are deemed paranormal in nature. Still, there are plenty of convincing anecdotal accounts in the historical record of individuals *and* animals that have left this earth only to return in a newly formed body. Evidence as to their previous incarnations number in the thousands, if not more. However, most of us (yes, even me) question that which is still so hard to work out within the reasoning left brain. It can be a difficult subject to fully grasp and understand. Therefore, perhaps it is best to leave the left brain out of it, and simply trust the signposts that have been put before us. In the case of Paws and Clover, we were gifted with more signs than we could have imagined!

Renowned animal afterlife and reincarnation expert Brent Atwater says, "...After the death of a pet and during your pet loss grief, hold faith in your heart that your pet's life force energy and love is never ending. The reincarnation process has been embraced by many of the world's oldest religions. Even if you're a skeptic, what have you got to lose by considering the possibility? If it's what you contracted to do, it might just be only a matter of time until your beloved animal companion returns to be with you!"

"I'm with my mother!"

In yet one more prophetic twist, within a week or so of Paws' passing, I had a vivid dream in which I was exiting our upstairs bathroom. When I opened the door, there was Paws as he always was, anxiously waiting for me to emerge from the bathroom. I recall my look of absolute shock. "How could you be here, you just died?!" He said (and he spoke to me as if human), "I had to come back because you were too grief stricken – I couldn't ignore it. But I can only stay for a little while (he said urgently). I have to go back because I'm with my mother."

At the time, although I was taken aback by his insistence about getting back quickly to be with his mother, I didn't question his desire to be reunited with her in the "afterlife." However, it wasn't until months later that I learned the facts about Clover's birth that in retrospect, I acknowledged, "of course he was with his mother – that's when Clover was being nursed *by* his mother!"

> *"Each soul or entity will and does return, or cycle, as does nature in its manifestations about man; thus leaving, making or presenting–as it were–those infallible, indelible truths that it –Life–is continuous."*
> -*Edgar Cayce Reading 938-1*

Animal reincarnation is just one more thread in the textile of infinite potential; the fabric of reality that we are still just beginning to process. Just because a phenomenon doesn't entirely fit within our understanding of reality, certainly does not prohibit that reality from existence.

As a footnote to this most curious play out of occurrences, I must make mention of a sequence of events that struck me as nothing short of synchronistic. During the passing of Paws and the (re)birth of Clover Paws, while all of this was unfolding, thousands, perhaps millions were watching on television, the memorial service for Whitney Houston, including my husband and me. We were sitting in the living room of my cousin Nancy Wilson, whom we had come to visit for a few days vacation after my interview with Dr. Goldberg in Los Angeles. *All* of this was happening at the same time! It was then that we got the call from the Veterinarian in Massachusetts – wanting us to be present for Paws as he took his last breath! The previous evening, I had made a silent request to Paws that if it was time for him to "go," that he give me a signal, knowing that there was a good chance that he would not last until we got back. We were scheduled to fly back to the east coast on the day he died! Shortly after we hung up with the Veterinarian, I recalled a dream that I'd had the previous night. I was at my home and I could hear Paws meowing. I went from room to room, looking for him but I could not find him. His "meows" were distinct but he was nowhere to be found! This was no doubt his sign to me that it *was* time for him to temporarily leave us, but it also signaled that his presence would never be fully gone.

Welcome *back* home, Clover Paws!

"*We are masters of ourselves, but not at the conscious level.*"
-Robert Monroe

Fourteen

❧ ❧

EXPLORING NON-PHYSICAL REALMS IN THE OUT OF BODY STATE

Continuing down the path of meta-normal states and the exploration of self, let us now look at a phenomenon known as the out of body experience or *OBE*. Considered together, we just may find that all of these events have the potential to transcend reality as we understand it and with it, the transformation of ourselves!

~~~

Sabreena was eighteen at the time, her sister a few years younger. Their parents were away for the weekend, so the two decided to pair up and sleep in their parent's bed while they were gone. As the younger sister lay fast asleep, Sabreena felt particularly agitated and restless. Resorting to counting sheep, she stared intently at the ceiling, hoping she would eventually dose off.

All of a sudden, Sabreena was looking at her sister from a different vantage point – from the very ceiling she only seconds ago found herself staring at while counting her way into the sleep state!

"Not only was I looking down, like I was on the ceiling, I actually felt like I was many feet higher than the existing ceiling. I could see my sister, sleeping on her side as she always did, and next to her *was me!* I had this strange detached feeling from the girl laying on the bed and yet I knew it was me – but this was the me looking at both of us from above. It scared the absolute crap out of me! I was disoriented and absolutely terrified. It was so quick. The moment I thought I was realizing what was going on, I had the sensation of falling, then I felt a thump and before you know it, I was *back* in my body. I'll never forget it."

The above was a real-life account told to me by a dear friend whom I've known for many years. In fact, she's repeated this story many times to me – still trying to search for some explanation as to what could have been going on. In the early years, when we were young and curious gals, we didn't know so much about something called the *out of body experience* or OBE as it is often referred. I of course, went on to study such anomalous events as part of my research into the *unknown*. Sabreena too has since become absolutely fascinated about the reality of such experiences.

OBE's were first introduced to modern culture by Robert Monroe, a former radio broadcasting executive who happened upon the curious phenomenon when he began having spontaneous out of the body journeys. Having no prior knowledge of such an occurrence, Monroe immediately began experimenting with techniques to control OBE's and later went on to develop various methods including his patented *HemiSync* technique to induce controlled OBE's. His 1971 book, *Journeys Out of the Body* brought the term "Out of Body Experience" to a wide audience and to those curious about the reality of their own similar experiences – the separation of consciousness from the physical body.

Like some of the other paranormal phenomena we've discussed in this section, OBE's rank among one of the most elusive aspects of the human experience, and yet the OBE is also believed to be among the most natural occurrences known to man.

William Buhlman, OBE researcher and experiencer, has authored several books on the subject, including *Adventures Beyond the Body* and *The Secret of the Soul*. He is well known for his groundbreaking research of out of body experiences worldwide, having gathered pertinent data to help us better understand the mechanics and features of the out of body state.

According to estimates obtained by Buhlman based on *The Secret of the Soul* published in 2001, over thirty percent of the population will have at least one OBE in their lifetime. I suspect that estimate is much larger at the time of this writing, given the fact that many more people are starting to report their own "paranormal" experiences as Rosemary Ellen Guiley stated previously.

Conditions such as an illness, injury or an unexpected trauma or even something as common as insomnia, similar to Sabreena's case, can trigger a spontaneous OBE.

Often, the experiencer will be caught off guard when the separation of consciousness from the physical body occurs. Many report feeling a full body vibration or hearing a buzzing sound or even voices, just prior to the separation. Invariably, the OBE will then occur and suddenly the person will see their own body from a different perspective in their immediate surroundings. Some have even reported traveling through walls or the ceiling of their home, and visiting friends or family located far from their current physical location.

I'll never forget a story my mother told me shortly after I had recently married and moved to New Jersey with my husband, nearly eighteen years ago.

"I was in my bedroom putting on makeup at my vanity, when suddenly I heard your voice. *'Hi Mommy,'* you said. I heard your voice as clear as day. It was coming from your old bedroom. You were there! And you know, I wasn't frightened by it – I was just caught off guard," she said.

What made this incident particularly curious to me at the time, was the fact that I had been practicing my meditation quite regularly while living in New Jersey. I remember on several occasions feeling myself moving into a very deep altered state during my sessions. Once I recall feeling as though my consciousness was indeed separating from my physical form. This was the first time I can remember having had what I could roughly describe as an OBE, but because the incident startled me so much, I immediately ended the meditation and resumed my daily activities!

I always found that comment "I wasn't frightened by it" very interesting coming from my mother, as she described this event. She was a very practical, grounded individual. When she would share stories with me that had a *mystical* or *unusual* quality to them, I knew she was absolutely serious, otherwise she wouldn't have bothered bringing it to my attention. She was not necessarily a vivid story teller – not known for it in any case, so when she would occasionally share odd occurrences that happened to her, I knew they were real for her! In fact, to this day, I truly believe that not only did she hear me speak, she *saw* me! There was a tone in her voice that told me she wasn't revealing the whole story! Unfortunately, I'll never know for sure what actually happened on that day.

Spontaneous out of the body experiences are apparently quite common and in most cases, when these little out of sync episodes occur, the temptation is to simply brush them aside, given most people have nowhere to put the experiences based on their existing belief systems.

William Buhlman feels adamant that not only should we embrace these experiences, but even incorporate what he calls *self-initiated OBE's* into our lives and spiritual practices.

Buhlman says, "The most powerful benefit of OBE's is that we have the ability to absolutely prove to ourselves that we continue [after death]. Number one - what are we? Where did we come from? Where are we going? What's our purpose? These things I feel can be discovered through out of body exploration. These experiences take us closer inward to our true nature and that's where the answers truly are."In addition to calming the fears associated with the death of the physical body, understanding that we continue to exist beyond the physical plane, Buhlman advocates utilizing self-initiated OBE's to reunite with loved ones who have passed over, and even meet those who've yet to incarnate into the physical form.

When I spoke with him during a phone conversation some time ago, he talked of having received letters from pregnant mothers who admitted having had communications with their unborn child in the OBE state! Repeatedly they reported meeting with who they described as "an adult soul," and how the soul was simply preparing to enter the physical world through the mother. Many times, the "unborn child" would give insight to the expectant mother on their connection in previous lives. This example denotes yet another piece of evidence for the authenticity of reincarnation!

Buhlman agrees that even in the last decade or so, more and more people are having psychic experiences, including out of body experiences. "Our society is totally obsessed with the outer form of everything," he says. Once we begin to initiate experiences that are outside of the physical framework, we will understand so much more about ourselves and yes, our magnificent potential!

It is not only possible to perceive other states of consciousness, but perhaps it would serve us quite well to practice initiating entry into these dimensions, in order to meet the increasing frequency for which our planet is now immersed. One stipulation, however – to explore beyond the physical is not necessarily an option to *trade* our presence on this earth for one that is *outside* of it. Many in the new age or spiritual movement have believed that to "get out of my head" and blast into the cosmos is the path to spiritual enlightenment. I don't agree. We are all here for a reason. By remaining anchored on this planet while in physical form, we have the opportunity to ground these amazing frequencies *into* the earth and throughout the planet while meeting the frequencies that mother earth is naturally achieving on her own.

As we begin to contemplate the clues these incredible experiences have to offer, let us not miss out on the enormous opportunity this new world has in store for us. The out of body experience serves as yet another brilliant access point to the evolution of mankind!

MUSINGS OF A NEW WORLD ~ II

Dear Diary:

 Last night I had the strangest dream. I was with my mother, almost twenty years deceased. We were in our old home – in the living room. The familiar Italian porcelain collectables, burgundy drapes and matching fireside chairs were as I once remembered them. My mother loved beautiful surroundings – objects d'art proudly displayed and plenty of comfortable seating to view them. We were sitting in those burgundy armchairs chatting away, when all of a sudden I said, "Mom – watch this…"

 I then lifted my left hand and waved it in an S-motion toward the Capodimonte figurine on the shelf in front of us, roughly six or so feet away. The female figure began to lift gently, gliding through the air. I continued to motion with my hands now guiding it over to the lower bookcase just to the left. As if magnetized to my motion – the figurine then perched itself on the top shelf of the case just to the right of our vintage family portrait.

 "It looks much better there," I said. She looked at me with absolute astonishment. "How did you do that?" I looked at her as if I didn't know what she was speaking of. "Do what?" "How did you move that piece? That's impossible!" I smiled at her playfully (of course she wouldn't know, she lived in the "old world.")

 I told her that everyone can do this now – "They call it telekinesis. It's a new technology we have. It makes things a lot easier to maneuver. It was discovered a few years ago and now everyone uses it."

 Once she managed to accept what I had just said, and what she'd just witnessed with her own eyes, she asked to know more about our technology and how it had changed our lives. I told her of how people are now able to travel great distances by thought alone, how we can communicate telepathically although verbal communication is still used, and how we can even visit with our loved ones in spirit – "Just as I am now – with you!"

 It all got strangely fuzzy after that.

I then abruptly woke up, confused by the scene but somehow feeling that it was real and very important. I had to write this down because somewhere in time, I know this will be the life we will all live – and I just got a firsthand look. How exciting!

SECTION THREE

THE CONSCIOUSNESS OF MANIFESTATION & ABUNDANCE

Conscious contemplation can be a refreshing process. The act of reflection, rather than reaction, to the ways of the world and of the human species *and* its potential, can provide momentum for the urge toward achievement.

We've mused over the psychological defects of society, acknowledged an over-abundant ego, rationalized reality, and conceded to collectivism as core to our societal struggles.

We have now taken the paranormal or *meta*-normal into serious account, and had the lucid realization that these are not quirks of nature, but rather central to its very foundation.

Traveling the road of recognition, we've had epiphanies along the way. We have decided to exert our spiritual sovereignty rather than hide it, embrace the act of revolution as a follow on to our evolutionary commitment – and we are now seriously contemplating the gestation of our having done so.

That's *a lot* of thinking indeed! Now, let us take a giant leap forward, into the world of ACTION!

To blame others or even ourselves about the challenges experienced is a futile endeavor. Rather, if we take responsibility, not for others but for ourselves, we will begin to transform the entire species, from leading by example.

Are we broke and broken, depressed and desperate, alone and agonized – fearful that our fate is solely dependent on the cooperation and granting from others? Or can we begin to take our lives into our own hands by seeding practices that will bear fruits for lifetimes to come, releasing us from the grip of karmic repercussion?

I think it is fair to agree that the latter is a far more palatable option!

How marvelous it would be if we knew – *really knew* that we held the keys to abundance squarely within our hands. Sort of like Glinda the good witch in The Wizard of Oz, when she says to Dorothy, "You've always had the power to go back to Kansas."

In this final section, *The Consciousness of Manifestation and Abundance*, we are *going back* to the fundamentally spiritual beings that I sense we once were.

When we utilize our imagination, engage the heart, dream big dreams and have the courage to take them seriously and to act upon them, we will see a transformation, not created for us by an outside source – but molded internally and manifested externally!

At the risk of sounding redundant, I can't help but reiterate that we *are* on the precipice of living in a New World – perhaps we are already here. Regardless of whether we view this as our current state or one that we are on the verge of living, why would we wait to see what the future will hold instead of capturing the magic of manifestation right now?

So let us allow for the present to coincide with the future as we conclude our set of musings on a confident note and start creating the reality that has always been well within our reach!

"He who has so little knowledge of human nature as to seek happiness by changing anything but his own disposition will waste his life in fruitless efforts."
-Samuel Johnson

Fifteen

❧ ❧

NAVIGATE THE SHIFT WITH BEHAVIOR MODIFICATION

American inventor and philosopher R. Buckminster Fuller once said, "If humanity does not opt for integrity we are through completely. It is absolutely touch and go. Each one of us could make the difference."

Of course one might consider this a dire prophecy. On the flip side, this could be a unique opportunity. Many have agreed that we are at a choice-point in our evolution. This "shift" of consciousness both planetary and even Universal is no doubt affecting us individually as well. While some are experiencing awakening and expansion, others exist within ultimate repression, conflict, and fear. But are these effects subjective? Moreover, *can* each one of us make the difference and in so doing, experience a reversal of fortune?

There is a statistic that has been pondered and discussed in many new thought circles, which postulate that if only the square root of one percent of the population made a conscious decision to change (in whatever direction it chose), that would be enough to shift the entire direction of the human race. Given that we have roughly seven billion people on the planet, that means it would take less than 9,000 people to modify an entire planet, hopefully for the better, kinder and more loving, and catapult us into a glorious new age. Even if these numbers are mere approximations, this is a powerful idea! We would be able to lift the quarantine of repression, whether self inflicted or super imposed – and then flourish individually and en masse!

How empowering it is to contemplate the innate wonders we all possess, but even more empowering it is to know that just a tiny fraction of the population can "bootstrap" the rest for the betterment of the whole. *That* is utterly amazing!

It Starts With Behavior Modification

We have heard it many times: *we* are the change we've been waiting for, but what does that really mean? Do we have the capacity *to* change? Of course we do! If we make an agreement and commitment with ourselves to take even baby steps in the direction of modifying behaviors that no longer serve us and embrace *and act on* new ones that do, we will no doubt begin to go with the shift, and not against it.

Here are a few things that can move us in that direction…

~ *Initiate Kindness* – It cannot be said enough, even the smallest acts of kindness can shift an entire mood for the one you've been kind to and to yourself. But there may even be greater implications. There is a term called *The Butterfly Effect* – the process by which a small change occurring in "non-linear time" can affect great changes across vast distances. Make a decision to initiate a small act of kindness on a regular basis – say leaving a quarter in a parking meter for the next car or holding the door open for the person behind you, and watch (or trust) that wonders will unfold.

~ *Pray for a Stranger* – I've found this incredibly powerful. When I converse with the Creator, often with a list of requests, I'll ask that a blessing be granted to someone I do not know. "Give someone good news today – something that could change their life for the better..." Understanding that indeed we are all part of one grand creation and are thus connected, by expressing good intentions for a "stranger" we are fortifying ourselves with blessings as well! For as it has been said, "There's only one of us here anyway!"

~ *Show Compassion and Empathy* – Sometimes, we are confronted with a person (a colleague, family member or stranger) who will exhibit behavior that is say, less than desirable. They may be mean and bossy, tricky and not trustworthy, jealous and competitive. Chances are, people who behave in this manner are conflicted in some way and for some reason. Rather than lash out in a knee jerk response, find a way, even if in silence, to feel love and empathy for that person and if possible, share a kind word to defuse their typical behavior. Both of you will have the opportunity to feel and be the better for it.

~ *Laugh Out Loud* – Laughter is well known to fire up endorphins that fill the body with life-giving properties. Make a commitment to have at least one good laugh a day (and not at somebody else's expense). Laughter is also *contagious*! How can we go wrong there?

~ *Honor Your SELF* – We live in a world of hierarchical systems. Somehow, man became habituated toward process and protocol, class and status. These have no doubt degraded the perception of the ultimate creation – *you*! No matter what and no matter when external messages may intimate otherwise, you must step out of this and honor yourself. Get quiet and contemplate who and what you are. Thank the Creator for you, even with all of your perceived flaws and mistakes.

Cherish your creativity and own your dreams. Absolutely no system can take that away from you!

~ *Make Conscious Choices* – You've heard the dictum, "don't believe the hype." The "hype" is escalating in subtle and profound ways – chiefly, through our media. With all of the convenience of technology we have at our fingertips, the push and pull to react and conform to "information" is strong. Remember that we always have a choice – especially if the information is not serving us. Make a choice to tune out what doesn't serve you. Take a nightly news diet. Instead, read a book, watch a lecture, listen to music or just be still. Bring yourself back to equilibrium by not allowing mass messages to interrupt or co-opt your flow. You have the choice. Take it.

~ *Give Thanks for the Experience* – As hard a pill as this reality may be to swallow, there is still something beautifully exquisite, grand and creative about all of its nuances. Perhaps we all agreed to be here at this pivotal time, to be a witness to all of its gradations. We have the opportunity to give thanks for being an integral part of this wonderful "project" – and perhaps by the simple act of giving thanks we will usher in an even greater spectacle than we could ever imagine!

These are but a few conscious steps each of us can take. No doubt, you have heard some semblance of these before, but I think it bears repeating and now more than ever! There is indeed an urgency of *Now!* For as Buckminster Fuller repeatedly indicated: "We are facing our final evolutionary exam. Is the human species fit to survive? Can we wake up sufficiently so that we can use our prodigious powers for the good of all, and for the many generations to come?"

Perhaps a modification in behavior beholds the correct answers for the evolutionary exam we are inevitably facing. Indeed, *we* are the change we have been waiting for!

*"If you do what you've always done, you'll get what
you've always gotten."*
-Anthony Robbins

Sixteen

❧ ୨୧

WANT CHANGE? BREAK YOUR ROUTINE

Routine – it's what makes up our lives. It's how we bring continuity to our day: make the bed, shower, get the kids off to school, go to work, come home, make dinner, go to bed and do it all over again the next day.

But for those who yearn for a life of transformation and positive evolution, staying committed to the dyed-in-the-wool routines we so dearly embrace, may not be the recipe that we are looking for.

Certainly there are some who can boast of a routine that may be far more exotic and interesting – or perhaps the routine is one that is designed to imbue spiritual quality into our lives, like daily meditation or prayer or yoga. All of these things done regularly are wonderful and build on the inner work that is essential for evolution, but do they need to be done the same way every day? Some may argue that they do, in order to be effective; but the bottom line is human beings are wired for routine and often resist giving up their precious rituals they've so proudly partaken in for so many years.

Indoctrination into an ideology that routine is a vital and fundamental part of our lives, is a notion adopted and played out by the masses. And yet there are so many that go through their lives repeating the same ritual day in and day out, no matter what the routine – but hoping for a change in circumstances, opportunities, and experiences. Life becomes a virtual feedback loop offering up the same pattern repeatedly.

The Triple R-Complex

The basal ganglia, the part of our brain that governs our daily habits is also referred to as the Reptilian brain or R-Complex, coined by physician and neuroscientist Paul D. MacLean. MacLean proposed that among other behavioral elements the R-complex is responsible for, ritual displays are among its chief constituents, thereby making routine a primary aspect to the human persona.

What I will refer to as the "Triple R-Complex," involves *repetition, routine and ritual.* This is a behavior that we all participate in at times. Although establishing a routine or ritual for some things may be satisfying on occasion, say preparing a traditional Thanksgiving meal and inviting the family over to participate every year, routine also has a tendency to discourage creativity. If we're repeating a tradition, year after year, how would we ever have the opportunity to experience something new and discover a fresh and exciting dimension of living? Instead of routinely stepping out of bed the same way each morning, why not try doing it differently – slowly roll your body into an upright position, take three deep breaths and then plant your feet firmly on the ground before you stand up, and then do it another way the next day. Even little things like this can ignite a shift in the reality we experience for that day – subtle and yet profound!

Could it be that on some level, if we mix up or break our routine, even temporarily, just when our brains or specifically the R-complex part of the brain is wired to give us the same experience in this perpetual feedback loop, we might trigger a shift in our outer environment or circumstances?

Did a minute change in routine trigger a lottery win?

Here's a personal example that I believe to be illustrative of breaking or even shifting routine, to make way for a different and gratifying experience.

Some time ago I was coming out of the shower and preparing to dry off. As is usually my routine, I picked up my bath towel, dried myself off, then as I started to replace it on the towel bar in the same position that I always do – washcloth on the left, bath towel on the right – something told me to reverse its order. I then placed the towel on the left and wash cloth on the right, making mental note that I had done so. The next day, I bought a lottery scratch ticket (something I indulge in rarely but do for fun ever so often). I also have a *habit* of not scratching off the ticket for a few days, but rather let it sit there until I'm ready to see what the ticket has in store.

This particular time, I went to get the ticket, scratched off to reveal the numbers and discovered I'd won $4,000! Just like that! Now, the rational mind (also a part of the R-complex/basal ganglia part of the brain) would quickly write off any connection between the two incidents. And although I certainly cannot unequivocally attest to a relationship between the two, the idea that the act of switching my towels triggered my lottery win became provocatively curious to me.

The timing was extraordinarily synchronistic and one that couldn't be ignored! It's also important to note that at the time I switched the order of the towels, I recall that I had been pondering the need for some change in my life – particularly financially! I had been researching the idea that even the smallest shift in routine could possibly cause the dimensionality of what we call reality to shift; our outer circumstances and experiences. And although I wasn't consciously thinking of buying a lottery ticket at the time, somehow that minute shift in my everyday routine may have opened the doorway for a larger reality shift to occur – to the tune of four thousand dollars!

As an aside, shortly after my lottery win, my husband revealed to me that he had recently had a dream in which I won a sum of money!

The R-Complex/basal ganglia part of the brain, that which I suspect governs our primary behavior that is rooted in structure and predictability, in some way knows how to filter out or discourage spontaneity and creativity – and it is for this reason that being conscious of our routines may be the first step in changing them up now and again.

Many cutting-edge quantum physicists advance the theory that the reality we experience is largely defined first internally, then decoded and expressed in the outer world around us and as such, is quite malleable. So it would make sense that if we are constantly engaged in the same behavior day after day, whether it is the way we get out of bed or organize the towels in our bathroom, *that* external reality will faithfully mirror the unchanged patterns we see in all aspects of our lives, even if they seem totally unrelated. The idea that repetitious behavior triggers repetitious reality becomes more plausible in this context. Thus, when we suddenly interrupt the signals in the brain that put us in daily auto pilot, we usher in the opportunity for our outer world to shift as well, even in the most mundane of switches.

While I wouldn't go changing towels and subsequently buying lottery tickets with the expectation of shifting your financial reality, (although if you do, I'd love to hear what happened), I would highly recommend you regularly examine your routine behavior and consider breaking it up now and then. You might find that the *ritual* of conscious recognition of your routine, is the only one you'll need to shift your reality in magnanimous ways!

"*In prayer it is better to have a heart without words
than words without a heart.*"
-Mahatma Gandhi

Seventeen

❧ ❧

HOW TO MANIFEST – LET'S GET TO THE HEART OF THE MATTER

Manifestation – it's on the minds and lips of most everyone today who studies, practices, and has committed to what we call "New Age Thought." *The Secret, The Power of Now*, and even classics such as Peale's *The Power of Positive Thinking* and Hill's *Think and Grow Rich* have u-turned many back to the origins of the "you create your own reality" edict, all proclaiming that our thoughts indeed have power *to* create. *Be* in the moment, *visualize* your dream reality and you can make it so. All of these mantras do have validity, but there is one key ingredient; perhaps the single most influential conduit to consciously creating our reality – *the heart*. But how and why is the heart of the human being – the magical rain maker, the instrument that has apparent non-local ability to pull "stuff" out of the ethers and into the 3D world, so core to manifestation?

First, it behooves us here to have a brief *think* about the law of attraction (LOA), whereby the assertion of *like attracts like* constitutes a fundamental tenet of the Universe. Another idiom – *Energy goes where attention flows*...we've all heard these phrases before.

As author and motivational speaker Lisa Nichols explains in *The Secret*, if you open an envelope expecting to get a bill, chances are that is exactly what you'll find. Conversely, if you have an expectation (the thought) of receiving a check in the mail – *voila*, your thought will manifest that long awaited tax refund that was three months late.

The real secret is: there is more to the story...

The Secret no doubt served as an important primer, indoctrinating millions into a novel way of contemplating their every thought. Many were inspired toward a proactive routine of abundance creation using picture scrapbooking and visualizing images, to stir up the energy to attract that very object or scenario.

Thoughts are a powerful precursor to creating one's reality, but if you look at instances in which thoughts, especially those which were redundant, created an outcome that seemed to correspond perfectly to the thought, what was behind it? *The feeling!*

Let's look at that. Have you ever taken notice of the feeling that comes every time you think of something that you may be anticipating? Something you are worrying about will bring a feeling of anxiety. Something that you are looking forward to like a vacation, will bring a feeling of excitement. It is a physical sensation that corresponds with the thought. If it's an authentic thought, you can't escape the feeling. Have you ever taken notice of how you *feel* when you receive news that may be shocking or unexpected? Your heart will emit a physical vibration – whether it's a pounding of fear or surprise or a fluttering when you're around someone that you are attracted to. How do you feel when you are in absolute gratitude about something that has been given to you that you've always wanted; or when you are absorbed in sadness from a tear jerker on TV; or the grief over a departed loved one? The heart has a physical sensation that is associated with *every* emotion that we carry – and that may be the key to how and why realities manifest via the heart.

The Heart Has Intelligence

In the perennial classic *"As a Man Thinketh"* by James Allen, he paints a beautiful and accurate word picture, conveyed in poetic tone, that is derived from the biblical text that says, "As a man thinketh *in his heart*, so is he." The intimation with this brief passage is that the heart apparently has some ability *to* think and have consciousness. From this passage we can deduce that "he" will become that which he thinks (feels, emotes) from the heart – his reality, circumstances, lot in life, et al.

An interesting study conducted by the Institute of HeartMath (IHM), a non-profit research and development organization out of Boulder Creek, CA, revealed that the heart is significantly stronger both electrically and magnetically than that of the brain, making it the single most powerful organ in our bodies. Simply put – this means it has *juice*! IHM, which was founded by Doc Childre in 1991, has made incredible progress through their many years of stringent research to determine that the heart indeed has intelligence and when properly tapped, it can facilitate changes on many levels, including reduction in stress levels, building greater resilience and optimizing overall well-being. Whereby some of these effects from a well-tuned heart may seem entirely realistic, could the heart also play a key role in creating the circumstances we experience in the physical world?

I spoke to the executive vice president of HeartMath, Howard Martin who also co-wrote the book, The HeartMath Solution with Doc Childre. He says, "The heart is the evolutionary imperative…it's an intelligence that's intuitive and high-speed." HeartMath's research, well-rooted in science, has shown that the heart is much more than a blood pump. "Science is our bridge. [It was] never designed to take the *heart* out of heart. It was designed to give it empirical understanding." And the understanding that has spilled forth in their studies is that it acts as a receiver-transmitter, communicating directly with the brain, and possibly influencing the reality that we experience in the external world. HeartMath's motto is, *"A change of heart changes everything."*

When you look at the field of possibilities – that which exists in the invisible realm that many have simply called "The Field," or "The Zero Point Field" – you can reason that somehow our consciousness; that which was born out of this field, is still connected to it – but there must be some sort of conduit or energy string that allows for that connection.

There are numerous accounts throughout history that have anecdotally yielded a curious phenomenon that point to the fact that many of our greatest inventions, artistic creations and prophecies were gleaned from some connection to this invisible albeit authentic realm. In nearly every case of these magnanimous manifestations, the experiencer will speak of being in a state or feeling of focus, euphoria and emotional abandon, which precipitated a synchronization with the Universe. Subsequently, the answer to a perplexing mathematical problem would be realized, or a flow of musical inspiration would dance its way onto a sheet of paper, culminating in a grand and complex symphony. Have you ever noticed how *you* feel while listening to a powerful symphonic piece, all instruments in perfect symmetry and harmonization? It's as if the original emotion that was used to put the pieces of the musical construct in order affected our own electromagnetic field – which of course, is received chiefly by the heart!

It seems that the heart acts as a transmission antenna of sorts, broadcasting via intense feelings, which strengthens the electromagnetic field and thus broadcasts the thought, intention and visualization into *The Field*. The Law of attraction then kicks in whereby the Universe acknowledges this broadcast, and rebounds it back into the physical realm in the form of the manifestation. This you might call the *law of reciprocity*.

The Harmonic Spectrum

In film maker and ecologist David Sereda's documentary *Quantum Communication*, the importance of coherent or harmonic sequence as it relates to the electromagnetic frequencies that the heart emits, is readily discussed. If you are in a state of fear, anger or sadness, the heart will produce an incoherent electromagnetic pattern and thus weaken the transmission of thoughts and feelings into the field, usurping our ability to manifest our positive desires. However, if one is centered within feelings of unconditional compassion, gratitude and love, the opposite will be true – thus creating a strong and harmonic resonance with this field. Cooperation then ensues and manifestation is primed to take place within one's physical reality.

In a telephone chat with Penney Peirce, author of the book *Frequency – The Power of Personal Vibration*, we discussed the impact that the raising of the earth's frequency is having on the quickening of manifestations, either consciously or unconsciously. She said, "I think [instant manifestation] is absolutely happening and I think in order to really get it to happen, we have to let go of thinking that things occur through

117

cause and effect. Time used to be linear and it's not anymore. Now it's spherical; it's all in the moment. If you get an idea, it's in there with you and all you have to do is put attention on it and keep attention on it. You don't even have to use *in*-tention because that's willpower and willpower doesn't work. Soft attention is what brings things in – love brings things in, not force. When you think of imagination like a little movie that you want to picture yourself in, you *get in* it and you *feel* it." (We will learn more about these ideas later in this book.)

Feel it! That seems to be the *secret* – key to manifestation of all kinds. Now there is science that appears to be backing this process. There is physics to manifestation, and its equation may very well reside within the heart.

So next time you set aside a few precious moments to practice manifesting, get to the heart of the matter – the force of materialization literally lies within!

"In art, the hand can never execute anything higher than the heart can imagine."
-*Ralph Waldo Emerson*

Eighteen

❧ ❧

STEPS TO MAKE HEART-BASED VISUALIZATION MORE EFFECTIVE

In the last essay we discussed some ground breaking research on how the process of creating our reality may lie in the *feeling* we put into our thoughts. The law of attraction is just that, *"a law."* Whether conscious or unconscious, your thoughts and feelings, especially those that are repetitive will manifest in perfect accord.

But to consciously manifest our true dreams and desires, we must begin to proactively "feel into" that which we desire. This is perhaps *the* most important point to understand! There are some exercises one can do to pump up that heart center to *feel* your way into creating your reality.

Here are some tips

~Simply practice "feeling" – Take notice of the physical sensation that is being emitted from the heart and how it corresponds with different emotions: excitement, anxiety, sadness, bliss, relief, etc.

~Notice the difference between these physical sensations. Does your heart pound when you hear shocking news? Is it warm and fluttery when you see someone you have a crush on? There are different energy vibrations associated with each thought and/or experience that you process.

~Differentiate between feeling that is coming from your

heart center (the 4th chakra) and the solar plexus (the 3rd chakra). Each is capable of "feeling" but the heart is said to be more connected with the "spiritual realm" and as research seems to indicate, is stronger electromagnetically.

~Practice recalling positive events in your life, and how they made you feel (the physical sensation coming from the heart is what you must focus on). Then, record them within your memory and use them regularly when going into a visualization session. Think of them as being in a box and stored away, but always ready and at your disposal.

~Think of words or phrases that may attract a positive emotional response from you. Repeat them often and amplify the feeling you get from the heart while doing so.

Put practice into action...

Here's one I used that seemed to *attract* something I had been wanting for so long – an iPad!!

At the time I didn't have the resources to spare to get this little "must-have gadget," but I wanted it SO much. I knew that it would be a joy to have during travel and for my writing – and a million other things! Rather than think-repeat-feel that *I couldn't* have it right now, I said over and over and over, *"I love my iPad!"* With each repetition I felt the sense of excitement at playing with my new device, showing it to my friends, getting on the plane with it in tow. *"I love my iPad...I love my iPad...I love my iPad!"* I felt every bit of it. I got excited. I could actually feel it in my heart...that sense of joy!

Not two weeks later as we were preparing to go on a business trip to South Africa, my husband announced that he had been wanting to make good on his promise to get me an iPad for my birthday (although my birthday was some months ago). He knew nothing of my little feeling-mantra I'd been practicing! Off we went to the store, and back I came with my new iPad. To this day – I'm still saying (and feeling) "I LOVE my iPad!"

I need to be clear about something – Although this little exercise was based on something tangible and fun that I wanted to manifest, the core of manifestation was less about manifesting an object and more about recognizing the process for *how* it manifests – this is where the true riches of understanding our manifesting powers are key!

~~~

~ Learn to *synchronize* thought and feeling. The art of manifesting is in the emotion that accompanies the thought. When you first have a thought, it might seem quite detached from its corresponding emotion. Almost like a recitation. But if you consciously decide to attach and *feel into* what that thought means, you will program your heart to have a resonance with the thought and it will become more natural.

~ Sustained Feeling – Once you've identified an emotion you like to feel, practice holding onto it – that literal physical sensation that you will feel coming from the heart. First try it for five seconds, then ten seconds until you can sustain a feeling for a minute or more. Once you can train yourself to maintain a feeling for a period of time, it will be easier to recall it back up.

~ Finally, put practice into action. Take the preceding steps and apply them to a reality you want to actualize. Take it easy at first. Work with *small* manifestations that are easy to imagine and feel. Write down the results. Notice the progress you are making in sustained feeling (the physical sensation coming from the heart) and jot down the manifestations that culminate from the intense feelings you've generated.

What a gratifying and empowering experience you will have. *Happy Manifesting!!*

"The dreamers are the saviors of the world. As the visible world is sustained by the invisible, so men, through all their trials and sins and sordid vocations, are nourished by the beautiful visions of their solitary dreamers."
-James Allen

Nineteen

❧ ❧

MAPPING MANIFESTATION THROUGH THE DREAMSCAPE

I have always found the notion of creating my reality from the sacred space of the ethereal, absolutely exhilarating! As potent as our five senses are – that which allow us to see, hear, taste, touch, and feel the physical world and to mold its many aspects to our liking – these faculties offer finite potential in and of themselves, compared to tapping the infinite universal sea that surrounds us at all times.

Our conscious waking reality, that which many of us feel is the only reality for which to build from, often gets priority over the subtle (and sometimes not so subtle) prodding that comes from the immeasurable waters of potential – or *the field* as some have called it.

The dreamscape is a most powerful entry point to this field and one that we traverse every night.

Those in modern society, particularly in the West, have made little investment in the value of the dream state. In fact, I've spoken to many people who swear that they *hardly ever dream*, let alone make a commitment to mine their dream existence to uncover answers to life's many questions.

It is well documented that most people over the age of ten years dream an average of four to six times per night while in the REM (rapid eye movement) sleep cycle – a time when brain activity can be on par with that of the waking state. It is in this state where some of our most powerful dreams, including

125

nightmares can bring on a life-like quality. How many times have we awoken from a dream and literally needed minutes to re-orient – to convince ourselves that we were "just dreaming?"

In many aboriginal tribes, dreams are a priceless instrument, used faithfully to solve challenges not possibly achieved during conscious waking time. The Australian Aborigines refer to *creation time* as "the dreaming" or "dreamtime," relying heavily upon the play of images, animals, and other totems to deliver pertinent information from the spiritual world.

Among various Native American cultures, the dreamscape is a sacred visionary portal and one that is still highly revered. Often accompanied by rituals such as fasting, or the assembling and usage of certain sacred plants, dreams were considered a necessary process for survival on this planet.

If you can consider that this Universe serves as an endless landscape of potential, in order to find that potential one would need a map to lead them down the right path. Dreams, as intangible as they may appear, can serve as that map guiding us to our destination.

We've heard of prophetic or precognitive dreams – a foretelling of an event or experience, sometimes appearing as an ominous message of something that is to come. I've long had an affinity to precognitive dreaming, whether massive in implication or the everyday mundane; this seems to be the metaphysical aptitude that has been bestowed upon me ever since I can remember. It was this ability, and one I share with many others who've told stories of premonitions through dreams that have attracted me to contemplate how dreams can be used to solve problems and to manifest our deepest desires.

There are countless anecdotes of record that tell of some of the world's most innovative inventions having been birthed from the dream state. Scientists and inventors like Albert Einstein, Nikola Tesla and even musician Paul McCartney have all claimed their dreams as the source of what was to become an historical innovation, breakthrough or award winning musical composition!

Not only have dreams provided solutions to challenging equations or inspired creativity for artistic purposes, the dreamscape has also been a trusted ally in life saving acts and in some cases, changed the course of history.

In Robert Moss' well researched book, *The Secret History of Dreaming*, he documents the amazing account of revolutionary abolitionist and iconic figure, Harriet Tubman and how her shamanic roots likely saved not only her own life, but the lives of countless others. She was thought to be "a dreamer and a seer." Hailing from a rich culture said to having originated in West Africa, her ancestral roots were steeped in spiritual travel and dream mapping. In addition to her initial psychic abilities, Tubman experienced a traumatic incident at the age of twelve that would accelerate her gifts and change the course of her life forever.

One day she found herself in between an angry slave owner and a young boy, who was trying to get away. The owner, aiming at the boy hurled a two-pound lead weight in his direction, missing him and hitting Tubman square in the forehead, splitting her skull.

It is reported that Tubman "died," but came back to life, encountering what is known as a near-death experience (NDE). Subsequent to this incident, Tubman began to have increased psychic abilities, including prolific precognitive dreams which ultimately guided her success in freeing hundreds of slaves, and lent invaluable assistance in their journeys through the famous Underground Railroad. The details of this incredible story are amazing to read – and too numerous to give proper attention to in this one essay.

Needless to say, as well documented as Tubman's life is, Moss says, "...the secret of Harriet Tubman's achievement has rarely been told." I must admit, as much as I thought I knew about this remarkable woman, I too knew very little about the integral role her psychic abilities played in the unprecedented adventure of her life, and yet I am not at all surprised!

This ability to map dreams for materialization of any kind is certainly not limited to individuals of high notoriety or those that some would call "exceptional." For what may have made these individuals special in the eyes of so many was in truth, their willingness to acquiesce to the dream state – and have the courage to bring their discoveries out of the world of the non-physical, and into the material realm.

I will never forget when my husband told me the story of how a dream not only foretold his eventually going to law school, but how the dream inspired him to write a thesis while there, that led him to being one of the winners of a prestigious national competition.

"I had a lot of things on my mind and was pre-occupied with what my next career would be. I wasn't necessarily happy with my current position, and wanted to advance my education and career choices. I remember having a dream, sort of lucid in state, in which I was writing a paper about copyright law – specifically about the process of digital music sampling and how it would impact the music industry. By the time I woke up, it felt as though this paper was already written. I immediately began to take copious notes and tucked them away for what I knew would be an important process on my next journey."

Soon after that, he decided to apply to law school, got

accepted to Vanderbilt University and graduated with honors, having authored *two* theses', one of which he wrote on digital copyright law – which garnered him second place with the coveted ASCAP Burkan Copyright Competition award!

Dream expert Kelly Sullivan Walden, who wrote the book, *I Had the Strangest Dream – The Dreamer's Dictionary for the 21st Century* relayed this story in a radio interview in April of 2013:

"There is a guy that I actually know personally who was in real estate and not doing well. He had a strange dream about a cell phone tower that bothered him. He thought, 'God these are ugly and they're cropping up everywhere!' In his dream there was a tree that sprouted up around this cell phone tower. He was so compelled by this that he woke up in the morning, sketched what he saw in his dream, patented it, and now is making millions of dollars, because he's the guy that created those fake tree designs that cover up these ugly cell phone towers that are everywhere....He was floundering – he wasn't doing well in business, then *poof*, there it is!"

Let us not underestimate the power of our dreams. They are truly available to us all! When we realize that it is within our grasp to consciously map the terrain of the dreamscape, we will have yet one more tool in our manifestation arsenal to see to it that our circumstances are not up for grabs in the hands of an accidental Universe!

There are numerous methods one can use to consciously map the dream landscape, but the one that I find most effective is to simply make a succinct and lucid declaration prior to going to bed either verbally or in written form (tuck the note in your pillow), then repeat the phrase as you fall off into the sleep state, allowing the phrase to be the last conscious thought you have before nodding off. Think of this process like planting a tiny seed in a mound of well composted soil – you may not know exactly when the seed will sprout, but certainly you will see it germinate in time due to the quality of the soil, that being likened to the terrain of the dream landscape. Make sure to feed and water your thoughts – repeat the declaration each night as if nurturing the seed to encourage germination. Most importantly, *let go of expectation!* As enticing as it may be to consciously craft the circumstances for which the manifestation is most likely to occur, resist the temptation to do so. By interfering with the manifestation process, you may inhibit a potential outcome that is way beyond what you can currently imagine, so leave it to do its own magic!

I fervently believe that the Universe is supportive to us and will meet us half way if we consciously engage its unlimited abilities. Dreams are but one channel, and a powerful one at that, which help constitute the riches of an infinite spectrum of which we are so innately connected!

"The senses are channels by which to interpret the infinitude of our being."
-The Author

Twenty

SENSING REALITY FROM
THE IMAGINAL REALM

In the last essay, we illuminated the abilities extracted from the invisible world as a valid and effective reality creation mechanism. But as we ponder our purpose within this physical world and the tools of the physical senses that certainly have a necessary function, how can we bridge these unique faculties to ground the invisible into the visible?

~ ~ ~

I am so grateful to consider author and intuition pioneer Penney Peirce a dear friend and mentor! Earlier, we contemplated her idea of increasing frequency on this planet and how we can leverage this progression to manifest a reality of our own choosing. I find that so much of her wisdom is fresh and insightful, *and* attainable!

As long as we make a commitment to contemplate the many nuances of potentiality that she and others like her have worked so hard to bring to us, for sure we will begin to diminish the learning curve and put our knowledge into practice!

Penney and I have shared many conversations, but one of my favorites, and one that struck me as somehow especially illuminating and very important, was our discussion about how we can use the five physical senses to process and create our reality. This can be tapped from what is called *the imaginal realm*. A term coined by French scholar and mystic, Henri Corbin, the

132

imaginal realm differentiates itself from that which is imaginary or contrived. It was his belief that the imaginal realm, from a metaphysical context, is composed of a "place" that is "above" the physical realm, although embodied ethereally speaking, in each individual. The imaginal carries its own unique frequency, coming from another realm – a more spiritual realm. Corbin designated what he called the imaginative consciousness: an organ that perceives this imaginal realm which he referred to as the "topography of these interworlds."

As we begin to wind down from our collection of contemplations about life and our unlimited potential, I thought it would be fitting to add what I'd consider to be a memorable exclamation point on our journey, to discover the amazing gifts of potentiality for which we've all been uniquely endowed.

Allow me to digress from our usual essay arrangement as in the preceding pages, and bring you in on this most fascinating discussion between Penney and me, as we discuss the imaginal realm and how we can link our physical senses with this incredible interworld to create a conscious reality right here on the physical plane...

~ ~ ~

Penney: It's very freeing to think that you can have *any reality you want.* If you can start to think it up, and get the ideas of it, and then engage with that much of it, and then start playing with it, then what happens with the imaginal realm is it starts to play back with you. It's like you have a playmate and you start to think, "Oh it would be great if I had some money." Then the imaginal realm would come in and say *"and* look what kind of house you could live in..." or "look at what would happen if you didn't have that house – where would you go?" (You could say) "Oh, I might travel around and stay with a bunch of friends…"

You can play with any combination of characteristics and try it on as a little movie. You can get the whole feeling of it and keep your attention in it. It will warp and change until it feels just right. And as it feels just right, and you keep your attention on it, it actually then gains life force. It drops down through the heavens or through the ethers and down through the brain from the abstract level at the top, then comes down toward your reptile brain where your body can recognize it. And then it suddenly just drops into form and becomes your living movie. It's all around you. And often you'll go "how did I get here?" …Because it happens quickly these days.

Alexis: So some people might say, "okay we're talking about creative visualization," but I think there's more – I happen to think that there's more to it than just a visual recitation of a scene that we like, but rather animating that scene and I attach the heart to it – *feeling into it* (as you have often said), really feeling what it would be like to, for instance live in a renovated home that you've always wanted and feeling what that's like – putting your hand over the smooth marble or granite on your new kitchen countertops, etc. Just really animating the situation…

Penney: What you're talking about is dropping it down through the mid-brain actually, which is vision at the very top, so it's the first level you get as an idea comes into you from the abstract realm – it becomes a vision. Then it drops and becomes tactile and you can hear it or smell it at the very bottom, as it gets to the reptile brain – you have this sense of taste and smell, but smell is a very animal-like core thing where it becomes *very* real. So as you drop it and *flesh* it out – literally through the senses, the body can really recognize it then. Visual is very mental, but when you get down to tactile and you hear things then you're getting more to the body. Now the thing just starts to take on the frequency of the physical plane...and there it is! So yes, it's much more than visualization.

Alexis: So you're saying that we need to process this scenario through each of the five senses that we have – visual, auditory, olfactory, etc...?

Penney: Yes!

Alexis: And repeat this process, right?

Penney: Yes. Round it out and flesh it out so that your physical self feels it...then it's real, then suddenly in your imagination it's real and then suddenly it's in your so-called "outer reality." There's no difference then between the imaginal-physical reality and the physical-physical reality. They're the same – they become the same!

Alexis: I've always felt that the imagination is one of the most powerful tools that we have as human beings.

Penney: That's right.

~ ~ ~

Penney has no doubt that we are now fast approaching what she refers to as "the intuition age" – an epoch of which we will depart the old information-based world, predicated on a very quantifiable linear framework, and enter a new world where at all times we stand at the center of an infinitude of probable presents, where we can create from and make choices fully of our own volition. This description is certainly befitting of Jung's mandala – representing the midpoint or center!

Penney maintains that it's *all* available right now. If we simply learn how to place attention (not in-tention, as she has said, because that implies force), we can get into that little movie that she described, and breathe life into the reality that we desire, while carrying it back from the imaginal and into the physical.

This is a most exciting vista that no one should opt out of in this new world that we now find ourselves in.

So, let's animate the imagination and experience the magic of ourselves, both physically and spiritually. The Universe is waiting for us to play it all out!

"To a great experience one thing is essential, an experiencing nature. It is not enough to have opportunity; it is essential to feel it."
-Walter Bagehot

Twenty-One

✌ ✍

FEELING YOUR WAY INTO
THE NEW WORLD

As we glimpse the calendar, we can't help but notice how fast time appears to be going by. When I talk to people from all walks of life, even young people, I hear comments like "I can't believe it's that time of year again"...No matter the season, it just feels that we've arrived here so quickly – where did the year go? Time as we know it simply seems to be speeding up, and there are some in the field of science who admit that this indeed is happening.

Much like previous years in recent history, 2012 is fast becoming a memory as well. Is this apparent speeding up of our time indicative of the new phase our world is about to enter? And even more important, are we speeding up along with it?

Among those who have researched the complex and fascinating calendar of the Mayan's, laboring to decipher its prophetic significance, many agree that their calendar system denoted the unprecedented exit of the fourth world and entrance of the fifth. December 21, 2012 represented that cross point; a trigger for sweeping changes, both visibly and invisibly.

Guatemalan researcher, historian and anthropologist Carlos Barrios has spent well over two decades studying the Mayan calendar. He maintains that December 21, 2012 became the start of a new era and thus a new beginning.

It is said that in this fifth world, we will see a fusion of polarities on all levels – represented as masculine and feminine. A blending or union of left and right, especially as it pertains to our own brain. Ego and intuition will finally make friends. The confrontation of the polarities will be transformed into one of balance, harmony, and love.

Imagine, in this new world we now have the ability to transmute all of the things that we do not prefer in our lives into those that we do? Imagine, in this new world we now have the power to manifest instantly with just our thoughts. In this fifth world, we will become five-dimensional beings – beings whose consciousness comes into full alignment with these magical powers; capabilities that we once possessed but had long ago become dormant.

Memories of a fully awakened consciousness will begin to blink back into awareness like the dream you insist you can't remember, but then throughout your day little snippets of the dream start to return back to you until you can fully recall the paradise you once dwelled in.

Let's try a little experiment. Let's visualize this new world. Let's visualize us in it, as we wish ourselves to be. Let's see if we can now utilize those manifesting powers with the tools of thought and feeling.

~~~

I want you to sit in a quiet space. Sit comfortably. Take a minute to clear your normal thoughts.

Now – close your eyes.

Take a deep breath – in through your nose and out through your mouth.

Take another – deep breath. Now, concentrate on your heart. Put your hand on your heart to focus your attention there.

Begin to feel the feeling coming from your heart. Think of someone that you love so very much or something that you hold so dear.

Concentrate on that.

Now, call up the feeling that thought brings you. Bring it directly into your heart.

Feel that sensation.

Hold on to that.

Keep focusing on your heart.

With every breath, center your attention on your heart.

Breathe deeply – in through the nose and out through the mouth.

Now, begin to form a picture in your mind of a life that is ideal to you.

You've just gotten word that you've been offered your dream job.

You've just met your soul mate.

You're about to board a plane to a long awaited destination you've always dreamed of visiting.

Whatever it is you prefer yourself to be and do. See it.
See it!

Focus on the feeling that your heart is bringing with this vision.

Can you feel that sensation?

Can you feel that energy that your thought is creating?
You are now living in a scene that you created.

...And it's *real!*

Look around you.

Where are you?

What does it *look* like?

What does it *sound* like?

What does it *smell* like?

What does it *feel* like?

What does it *taste* like?

I want you to feel this reality that you've created with all your heart.
Feel it!

Animate it with all of your five senses and bring it into your body.

Feel the smile that is starting to form on your lips because you're finally where you want to be.

You're excited!

Feel the reality of this scenario you created.

Now – Take a deep breath – in through the nose and out through the mouth.

Check your heart again. How do you feel?

Sit with this reality you've just created for a few minutes until you feel you've fully aligned it with your consciousness. This is real – *for you.*

Now just sit and relax.

Slowly open your eyes. *Slowly.*

Re-acquaint yourself to your immediate surroundings.

~~~

Commit to calling up this reality you've created and focus on it with your heart each night just before you fall into sleep. Our thoughts are most potent when we carry them into the sleep state (as we discussed in *Mapping Manifestation through the Dreamscape.*) You can certainly create and visit this reality in your dream state as well.

You've now just taken the first step to manifesting your reality in the new world – the fifth world. This is the world beyond 2012. Partake in all the gifts it has to offer!

"It is no use walking anywhere to preach unless our walking is our preaching."
-St. Francis of Assisi

Twenty-Two

❧ ❧

NOT SO FAST – PRACTICE WHAT YOU PREACH!

In September of 2013, the bottom dropped out! After a relatively optimistic summer, much of it spent penning and refining the words and sentiments you've just read, several promising opportunities on the horizon for my husband Derek and I and our business, all came to a screeching halt – just like that!

The world – our world, took on a gloomy and frankly frightening hue. Reality had shifted in an instant and the future wasn't looking so bright. With one insight which came to us on a Monday morning while my husband was dashing off to a meeting, he said angrily while walking out of the door, "This isn't going to happen!" While I will spare you dear reader, from bringing you to the weeds of what *this* denoted, let's just say, that which we had been "banking on" didn't pan out – at least not at that time – and for that we found ourselves in instant quicksand, wondering how we would make ends meet, keep our home, continue to exist with any semblance of decency, or continue to exist at all. Ergo, *it got ugly*!

How could I have worked so passionately and laboriously to put the final touches on what would be my newest creation – these *Conscious Musings,* only to have it lost? And even if I could resurrect it, how could I speak from a place of altruism, authenticity and certainty and sit well with it all? How could I preach these truths without the courage of my own

145

convictions? I couldn't!

Granted, it's far easier to let's just say, sit from a perspective of relative ease when delivering sentiments to those you'd like to inspire. I thought, "I've seen and experienced a lot in my years; traveled the world, met and interacted with people from all walks of life. I'd been discerning, introspective, honest and I'd clearly seen the world as it is, vs. the world as it could be. I've had my share of *dips* and *curves*, and many epiphanies because of them. I'm certainly ready to impart what I've learned (and am still learning)." Perfect, right? The Universe said, "Not so fast!" Actually, it was necessary for me to be brought to my knees and look back up from a true perspective of ground zero!

Things got so dire, I was not able to compile the funds to complete the book publishing process on my scheduled date – I had to shelve it, wait until things got better. And then the realization came: "The book's not finished yet!"

Alas, this is a story that *had* to be told. An ending to a real life script that said, "*You* must be the personal embodiment for which you speak."

In fact, that is just what my friend Penney Peirce said to me three months previous to the calamity in June, while visiting us at our home and gifting Derek and I with a reading. She said, "You must use your personality as the tool for getting things done...you must show up as yourself, use your personality as the vehicle to show others, *I am the personal living embodiment of...*"

Although I had no idea how this need would manifest, it is clear to me now at this writing that I had to be the personal living embodiment of all that I'd penned in this volume. For it would be necessary, unbeknownst to me at the time, to walk my talk in ways never imagined. It wouldn't happen any other way. And so, the Universe presented me with the experience to speak from, and it told me, "*Do* or *bust*!"

This became the critical epiphany. A watershed moment to be sure!

And so the adventure commenced.

They say that we stand on the shoulders of giants. In my case, I had to stand on the shoulders of all that I'd written, felt, breathed and been convicted by. I decided to do just that. I knew I had to step up my game as far as taking my own advice was concerned. Honestly though, there were times of despondency and fear – emotional anxiety beyond measure. With this I got to experience a sense of hopelessness I'd not known before. But then I said, *this* is what I'd so eagerly counseled others about – and now I've got to work through this process myself – take back my power and not allow perceived external circumstances take me down in a cauldron of fire. So, I meditated more, I talked to myself *OUT LOUD*. Contemplated and questioned like never before. I shouted to those that would listen (in the invisible world, that is), "What is happening? What do I need to do? Will you assist me?" It spoke and I listened. I took the cues of the Universe, metaphorical as they would come, although I knew it would speak to me if I asked. And so the dialogue between me and the Universe began. Some strange things happened during those turbulent, anxiety ridden months. And they were all significant. I'd committed to being open to the messages, because I knew they were there, if only I looked and listened AND took action! They came in dreams, in peculiar, beautiful, powerful, and sometimes humorous synchronicities – just enough to keep sane while riding out this storm.

Jumping on the Synchronicity Highway

As I watched our external reality go down a highway that seemed to be leading to inevitable misfortune which in the end threatened dire consequences, I began by refusing to accept that as our fate. I've known most of my life, felt intuitively, that we all have the ability to literally make our reality, and if this is so, then the reality that we may find ourselves in at any given time can also be shifted to another that is more desirable. But it had to start with a plan. And so I tapped the invisible world to help me on my new course. Fortunately, Derek was game to come along as well. After all, what would we have to lose?

I began by becoming acutely aware of my surroundings; all things happening around me – in nature, in conversations with others, in books and on TV, virtually anywhere that messages might show up, to help us navigate out of our current state. And so they did. In fact, looking back in retrospect, the synchronicities – those meaningful *coincidences*, began speaking to me *before* the crisis had officially begun. Here's one that I will never forget…

It was mid-August and I was talking with my cousin on the phone, sitting in our living room, peering out a large picture window overlooking our backyard and the wooded landscape beyond it. As I'm speaking with her, all-of-a-sudden a small bird came flying out of nowhere, headed straight for the window and right smack at my face! The bird slammed into the window, making an awful sound, startling the heck out of me. It happened so fast I was caught off guard, but when I could settle down enough to gather myself, I knew someone would have the grim task of collecting the dead bird beneath the window on our patio. Frankly, I was too squeamish to take on the job, so I summoned Derek to check out the scene and gently dispose of the bird. Several minutes later, he came to me and said, "There's no bird down there. I've looked everywhere. It's not there!" That was impossible. I saw how fast that bird was coming and how hard it hit the window. The bird had to be dead, or at least seriously injured. No bird to be found!

In Trish and Rob MacGregor's thought provoking book entitled, *The Synchronicity Highway*, a term they've coined to describe a realm that can be traveled, along with all the magic and strangeness of Alice in Wonderland, they say, "Synchronicity is subjective, dependent on the perspective of the observer. If you don't recognize a coincidence as meaningful, it's not synchronicity. It's just a coincidence."

I'd always considered myself quite aware of synchronicities around me, so I sensed at the time that there was some message implicit in this off-chance occurrence; however, it wasn't until weeks later that it began to take on a more inspirational though ominous tone. It said: *Despite the fact that it feels like you're hitting a wall, (or will be) you will still get up, keep going, and eventually fly!* And then, yet another stunning realization occurred to me: The bird came so quickly at me; it took me totally by surprise, as did the inevitable crisis that we would find ourselves in come September! With this, our trek down the *Synchronicity Highway* officially began.

Another point that Trish and Rob make in their book is that once you begin to recognize the presence of synchronicities, it seems to trigger even more. However, the experiencer must commit to sharpening what I call "subtle acuity." Synchronicities can be extremely vague, given the fact that they can happen in the most unwitting of ways. I knew I'd have to hone my gaze, become almost hyper-sensitive to my surroundings, and so would my husband. We did.

This wasn't our first journey down the synchronicity highway. We had a little test drive as fate would have it, some years previous! In March of 2008, Derek and I had been on a business trip in London. We were dining with a colleague – another entrepreneur who'd had his share of bumps and bruises, when all of a sudden he launched into a sobering discourse, instantly taking on the character of father and advisor, warning us urgently how bad things can happen to entrepreneurs. "It's a brutal world out here. I've been through it – almost lost my business, lost my customers *and* my wife, in the process." But then he said, "As long as you keep your focus on what you're doing and your faith in God and each other, you'll be fine." Why had he felt the need to go down *that* highway? There was nothing to precipitate the discussion. It was completely out of context. All seemed to be fine at the time. In fact, after dinner as we were riding the elevator together up to our hotel rooms, he became visibly awkward, embarrassed in fact – as if he didn't know where this sudden need to impart this wisdom came from.

Less than one month later, much to our surprise, our small business lender decided to pull out of their commitment to us, leaving us in a free fall and putting us on another path altogether. How would we know? As synchronicity would have it, the writing was on the wall in a lovely French restaurant in London, less than one month previous!

The "London story" was so strange in fact that the Boston Globe decided to include it when they featured my husband and me for a piece on the adventures of married couples in business – of whom they dub "couplepreneurs." This incident was our first shared experience about the mystery and magic of synchronicities and how if recognized they can serve as a catalyst to weather the storms of life!

We often reflect on that most profound and quirky incident, and it has served us well in understanding the miraculous way the Universe uses all matter of physical life to convey its messages, *if* you agree to take notice! So the synchronicities continued post September 2013, but so did the crisis. Nothing of note had transpired to signal to us we were turning the corner. Still the signs and symbols were unrelenting and we made the decision to use these messages as our ultimate compass, determined to ensure that the end result would be success...however that would look!

11:11

Synchronicities are often seen through the repetition of numbers, acting as a language all on their own. The 11:11 phenomenon, though elusive in its significance, has become an enigma that millions of people on this planet have been experiencing in recent years.

We both began noticing the 11's back in 2005, during a previous transitional phase in our lives. I'd covered the 11 story in some of my prior writings, as an attempt to explore why this master number had become so ubiquitous in the human experience. Eventually for us though, these 11 sightings began to subside. They would disappear from our lives as mysteriously as they showed up. Why? We honestly didn't know. However, as if on cue, I began to notice them again, right smack in the center of our season of crisis. I hadn't thought to mention it to my husband, but I certainly filed it away as yet another synchronicity of significance; another *shout out* from the Universe saying, "I'm speaking to you!" Then one day as we were taking a drive to ease the daily tension, it occurred to me to ask Derek if he'd been seeing the 11's again.

"Yes!" he admitted with a pitch of trepidation in his voice. We both looked at each other and shook our heads.

Rob and Trish MacGregor touch on the 11:11 phenomenon in their book, stating, "The message of 11:11 seems to be about the evolution of consciousness, that you're being ushered into a greater reality, the flow of Universal energy. It can also act as a warning and as confirmation."

This last bit: "warning and confirmation," caught my attention. Sure we were being warned via the synchronicities all about us, just like the gentleman who warned us of imminent challenge while dining in London, or the bird smacking into the window. But the confirmation of *change* and the idea that if we engaged the Universe, it would be willing to point us toward a greater reality, was also a clear signal to me. Either way, I chose not to analyze the resurfacing of 11's too much, but just continue to pay attention and allow the signs to guide us as we'd requested.

Dream Check-Ins

The dreamscape has always been a valuable asset to me on my quest to understand the terrain of life and the true nature of reality. As we discussed in *Mapping Manifestation through the Dreamscape*, dreams can act as a means to solve problems that might otherwise be unknowable. Keeping this in mind, I thought it would be impossible to *not* include our dreams as a powerful ally to help us along this highway, and to a safe and successful destination.

I'd also enlisted the power of daydreams and visualizations to see if we could somehow link our waking visions with our night time excursions as a means to shift our physical reality.

Each morning Derek and I would share our remembered

dreams over coffee, compare notes and see if they might be spelling out a scenario or solution that would help us out of this tumultuous period. Needless to say, there were many possible scenes that we'd dreamt, any of which could play out in our waking reality. There was a common denominator however in our collective dream experiences; a message of reassurance that we would *not* be enveloped by the quicksand of crisis and yes, we would make it through! We chose to trust it.

Although the dreams, the uptick of 11's and other notoriously nebulous synchronicities were faithful in their omnipresence, still we'd not received any specific answer as to how this crisis would break. Alas, we just had to trust that it would reveal itself in the best way and at the perfect time.

Reaching the boil point & coming to a head!

As we approached the holiday season, a time that we both usually embrace and enjoy to the fullest, it became clear to us that this year would probably have a very different tone. We'd become nearly depleted of funds, and no visible signs that would change anytime soon. And now the holidays? Certainly, having money was not the be-all, end-all to having a "nice" holiday. This was never the case for us. But feeling the financial pinch and the uncertainty of the future wouldn't make it especially cheerful either. Nonetheless, we would make it magical in our own unique way. And yet, admittedly while being on the verge of depression, would I even want to decorate the home, listen to holiday music or visit friends? I just didn't think I could muster the spirit this year. On top of that, my husband began to grow increasingly worried as did I, that a bump that he had been noticing on the back of his head had grown unusually large.

Curiously, the presence of this knot on his head became more visible just as the crisis we faced became more pronounced. He'd been watching it for some time, but neglected to have it looked at, although he felt pretty confident that it was due to some ingrown hair or mishap from shaving, until one morning he came downstairs and showed me the bump. It was nearly six centimeters in size and becoming somewhat painful, seemingly overnight. *Murphy's Law* was certainly kicking into high gear. What would be next?

Ironically, it was only days before that we had been talking to a friend who had felt the need to console us during our difficult financial period. "You'll get through this. What's important is that you have your health. That's what matters." And now, that could be threatened too?

Fortunately, after having it looked at, followed by a steady course of antibiotic treatment and compresses, it was determined that it was a boil that had come to a head and desperately needed to be drained. It did, and now all is well.

Once under control and we both were able to breathe a huge sigh of relief, I asked my husband if it had dawned on him that this little health scare was somehow symbolic of all we were experiencing? Did we reach a boiling point? Has it now come to a head? His answer – "Absolutely!"

We both sensed that the turning point was near!

Harnessing Holiday Magic!

With an attitude of gratitude for what turned out to be nothing but an annoying boil, this incident and its end-result managed to renew our sense of hope on so many levels. We knew it carried its own significance, and we'd chosen to build upon the momentum.

It was maybe two weeks before Christmas – a time that we'd considered magical ever since we were both children. It occurred to us – if we believe this time to be special in some enchanting way; a season of miracles, might we be able to tap that magic in our hearts? Can we ignite that holiday charm to help us down the final stretch of highway?

We both committed to calling up the holiday spirit. We decorated the house top to bottom, filled the air with music, and relished in the blessings of warmth, of love and of each other.

We then sat together and we prayed out loud, "Dear God, would you show us your magic? Will you spark in us the cheer and the treasure that we know lives within us? Will you send us a Holiday Blessing?" We then gave thanks for all that we had and then lovingly let our request go.

Merely days later, an unexpected sum of money showed up, then another and another…just like that! Simultaneously business began to pick up…*yes, during the holidays*! Doors began to magically open and at this writing, they continue to do so!

Something else happened. When I decided to check in with my surroundings, scanning the landscape that had been set before me, something occurred. I hadn't been seeing the 11's with the same frequency as in previous days. I then checked in with my husband, hoping against hope that his assessment would be the same. Affirmative!

As much as we'd like to know the significance of a repeated sign when it actually happens, sometimes it is necessary to notice the absence of it in order to realize its message. In our case, the *fading* of 11's was guiding us as well!

While we've acknowledged that the ultimate destination may yet to have been reached, the journey has brought us well over the mountain – and for that, we are immensely grateful!

For all intents and purposes, the drought for the time being has ended, but the powerful message that we received while traveling this synchronistic highway continues:

...JUST TRUST!

Musings of a New World ~ III

Dear Diary:

Although I usually dedicate my writings to the telling of my extraordinary night time dreams, I thought I'd share a "waking vision" and the amazing aftermath that succeeded!

I was sitting at my desk at work, bored from the monotony of the daily grind and admittedly growing more irritated about the environment I face each day. I found myself doing a bit of daydreaming. I'm not ashamed to admit that I do daydream a lot! But this time, it was different. I was somehow transported to a scene that felt so real to me.

I've always wanted to travel the world – to see places and meet people I've never experienced before. I'd dreamt of somehow finding a career that would allow me this experience – you know, the "dream job." But this doesn't happen in the real world. Besides what could merit my doing such a thing? I've seen people on TV who travel around the world and report back to us "regular folks" about ancient temples and historic discoveries, touring European countries to sample the food from local eateries and then teach us how to prepare them at home. They swim with the dolphins at exotic tropical locations and report back to us about their unique experience.

I'd salivated at the idea that such a "job" could really exist, but I would eventually let it go, relegating it to my bucket list of wishful thinking.

Then something really odd happened. While I was daydreaming, out of the blue, I heard the sound of a jet revving up its engine, ready to receive its passengers. I was in line to board that plane! I could see the gate open and the attendants motioning us forward to hand them our boarding passes. I could feel my heart beating in anticipation of boarding that flight – it was a good feeling; a sense of pure excitement that I was going on a journey I'd always fantasized about. It was so real – the smell of it, the sight of it, the feel of it.

After a long overnight flight, there I was, on another continent. A pleasant young woman stood waiting to greet me, then escorted me to a waiting car. While en route to our destination, she handed me a sheet of paper – an itinerary of some sort. I glanced at it and acknowledged the schedule, then...

My boss walked toward my cubicle and the daydream abruptly ended!

The following evening, I got a call from an old friend whom I haven't heard from in years. He had learned of the recent opening of a position overseas that required an individual who was fluent in both Spanish and English, and would have the ability to travel frequently to other parts of the world. He thought I was perfectly suited for it and wanted to know if I'd be interested in applying for the job.

Needless to say, I am now jotting this entry from my new apartment in Spain. I've relocated to a small coastal village in Catalonia called L'Ametlla de Mar and I am loving every bit of it!

I don't know how this all actually happened, but I have a funny feeling that this imagined vision set the stage for this new phase of my life. I am so incredibly grateful for the fact that I never abandoned my favorite past time of day dreaming. So much for "the real world!"

FINAL CONTEMPLATIONS

❧ ৯

"Stop looking for the guru 'out there.' They are no measure to the guru you already know."

-The Author

Y*ou* are the guru, the shaman, the light worker, the creator – of your own life. And it is my sincerest conviction that you are here to express each of these qualities, fully, completely and generously. We are all on a magnificent journey. But the goal to life may not necessarily lie in reaching the destination, but to embrace that journey – to explore, grow, share and live!

We are the alchemists. We have the ability to turn scrap metal into gold, challenges into triumph, fear into love.

The alchemists of old also realized the cyclical process of creation and destruction, light and shadow, and the necessity to engage each action in order to shift from one reality to another, oscillating to and fro. Polarity and duality do have their purpose as well. Like the quantum physicist who observes reality from a subatomic level, the wave and the particle co-exist; it simply depends on the state of surrounding conditions that will determine which role it will play.

Our conditions are changing drastically, both internally and externally. Ultimately one will mirror the other. If we can muster the strength and conviction to shift our internal reality out of a state of deficiency and embrace our inner gifts, our outer circumstances will pour forth with abundance.

This is and always has been a planet of pure bounty – I've sensed this even from childhood. It is now time to acknowledge its life-giving properties, in order to reap its benefits on a scale yet to be experienced in the modern age!

Gratitude...

I am eternally grateful to all of those individuals, both living and deceased, mentioned in this short volume of essays that helped to further illustrate the points highlighted throughout our journey here:

James Allen, Brent Atwater, PMH Atwater, Carlos Barrios, David Bohm, Gregg Braden, William Buhlman, Edgar Cayce, Doc Childre, Henri Corbin, Leo Deis, Albert Einstein, Ralph Waldo Emerson, R. Buckminster Fuller, Vincent Gaddis, Dr. Bruce Goldberg, Judith Guggenheim, William Guggenheim, Rosemary Ellen Guiley, Cissy Houston, Dr. Jane Katra, Airi Kivi, Neil Kramer, Rob MacGregor, Trish MacGregor, Dr. Paul D. MacLean, Howard Martin, Paul McCartney, Terence McKenna, Lynne McTaggart, Robert Monroe, Robert Moss, Lisa Nichols, Penney Peirce, Jane Roberts, Peter Russell, David Sereda, Dr. Bernie Siegel, Bernadette Soubirous, Dr. Ian Stevenson, Michael Talbot, Nikola Tesla, Russell Targ, Harriet Tubman, Dr. Jim Tucker, Kelly Sullivan-Walden, William H. Whyte, Jr., David Wilcock and Nancy Wilson. *...With sincere gratitude!*

Let us not quiver or squabble over the world as it *was*, for this new world wears a broad smile on its face, ready and willing to welcome us with open arms. Do not turn your back on this invitation. Do not deny its beckoning for your embrace. Meet this new world with exuberance and joy and relax into a space that has no boundaries.

Now, let us go confidently on the path of our dreams – Let us go beyond *musing the dream* and at this moment, live it!

Let us express unconditional love for ourselves, share our new found wisdom with others and know that we and the Universe are after all, *One*.

Out of the dark abyss, there emerged a pair of outstretched hands. Gently moving toward me, I squinted, blinded by the hazy light that surrounded its shape, I knew not what it wanted with me.

I could not move. I could not speak. My eyes became affixed to what materialized in its gentle palms. The hands came closer, cradling its contents.

There it was — the sphere of life, the nucleus that I had been missing from for so long. Its vibrant colors and intricate shapes penetrated my being with a purpose that I could no longer ignore. I had a vivid remembrance that this was once me.

Now it is being returned to me with the promise of transformation.

This time, I shall partake in its promise and never look back. This time I will accept what these hands offer, the promise of me — as I was meant to be!

-Alexis Brooks

References

One: Dichotomy of Consciousness and the Precipice of Change

Victims of the Attack – Martyrs for Meaning by Alexis Brooks: Source: OfSpirit.com, 2001: www.ofspirit.com/alexisbrooks1.htm.
The Attack: What I Witnessed on the Inner Planes by Dr. PMH Atwater, 2001: www.cinemind.com/atwater/resources/PDFs/Articles/ATTACK.pdf.
'Bank of Happiness' Lets Customers Deposit and Withdraw Good Deeds by Eleanor Goldberg. Source: The Huffington Post, 2013: www.huffingtonpost.com/2013/07/18/bank-of-happiness_n_3617833.html.

Two: Experiencing the Turning Point – Trepidation or Transformation?

The Mystery of 2012 – Predictions, Prophecies and Possibilities by Gregg Braden (and other contributors including Peter Russell). Sounds True, Incorporated, 2009.

Three: Death of the Ego – R.I.P.

Monster.com commercial spot *"When I Grow Up"* – 1999.

Wall Street. Film by 20th Century Fox, directed by Oliver Stone, written by Oliver Stone and Stanley Weiser, 1987.

Terence McKenna (writer, philosopher). Quotes from various resources including, *The Transcendental Object at the End of Time* by Terence McKenna, www.hiddenmysteries.org/health/research/transobject.html.

Four: The Emergence of Individualism

The Individual and the Nature of Mass Events by Jane Roberts and Robert F. Butts, Amber-Allen Publishing, 1995

"Groupthink" by William H. Whyte, Jr., Fortune Magazine, 1952.

Neil Kramer, *The Path of One*, 2011: www.neilkramer.com/the-path-of-one.html.

David Bohm, quotes excerpted and derived from a. Michael Talbot interview (New Dimensions, see below) and b. Talbot's book, *The Holographic Universe*, respectively. Additional reference: *Wholeness and the Implicate Order* by David Bohm, Routledge; Reissue edition, 2002.

Self Reliance; an essay by Ralph Waldo Emerson, originally published in 1841 and excerpted from The Complete Essays and Other Writings of Ralph Waldo Emerson. Random House, Inc., 1940.

Five: Rationalizing Reality

The Holographic Universe by Michael Talbot, Harper-Collins, 1991.

Six: No Revolution Without Evolution

Occupy Your Self! – *Personal Spiritual Development*, a documentary by David Wilcock, November 2011: www.divinecosmos.com/start-here/davids-blog/992-videooccupyyourself.

Seven: Spiritual Sovereignty

The Unfoldment by Neil Kramer, New Page Books, a division of Career Press, Inc., 2012.

Eight: The True Nature of Reality – Do We Really Know the Whole Story?

"Lisa's Story" – A personal account delivered to the author while vacationing in Aruba – 1998.
The Celestine Prophecy by James Redfield, Warner Books, Inc., 1997.
Conversations with God by Neile Donald Walsch, Book 1: G. P. Putnam's Sons; First Edition edition, 1996.
The Seat of the Soul by Gary Zukav, Free Press, 1990.
Talking to Heaven - A Medium's Message of Life After Death by James Van Praagh, Signet; Reissue edition, 1999.
Mysticism and the New Physics by Michael Talbot, Penguin Books; Revised edition, 1993.
Michael Talbot interviewed by Michael Toms, New Dimensions Broadcast, recorded 1991.
Miracles of Mind – Exploring Nonlocal Consciousness and Spiritual Healing by Russell Targ and Jane Katra, Ph.D. New World Library; 2nd edition, 1999.

Hello from Heaven by William Guggenheim and Judy Guggenheim, Bantam Books, 1995.

Remembering Whitney – My Stories of Love, Loss, and the Day the Music Stopped by Cissy Houston with Lisa Dickey, Harper Collins, 2013.

"Nancy's Story," – A personal account delivered to the author, circa 2009.

Nine: Transcending the Rules of Reality

Michael Talbot interviewed by Michael Toms, New Dimensions Broadcast, recorded 1991.

Mysterious Fire and Lights by Vincent H. Gaddis, Dell Publishing Co., Inc., 1967.

Love, Medicine and Miracles by Bernie S. Siegel, M.D., HarperCollins, 1988.

Ten: Geophysical Phenomena and the Thinning Veil

Leo Deis' story, *"Regina Man Sees Broom Defy Gravity – Stand on its Own,"* Calgary Times, 2012.

Rosemary Ellen Guiley, a conversation with the author, 2012.

"The Sun Does a Flip," NASA Science, 2001: www.science.nasa.gov/science-news/science-at-nasa/2001/ast15feb_1/.

Awakening to Zero Point, the Collective Initiation by Gregg S. Braden, Sacred Spaces Ancient Wisdom,. Second Ed., 1997.

The Intention Experiment by Lynne McTaggart, Altria Books. Reprint Ed., 2008.

Eleven: Is Paranormal the New Normal?

Personal account *"The flying lid,"* told to the author, 2012. Rosemary Ellen Guiley, a conversation with the author, 2012.

Twelve: Birth-Marking Past Lives

"Cloy's Story," as told by Dr. Jim Tucker, published on You Tube in 2012: www.youtube.com/watch?v=h6M-nXjh_9I
"Birthmarks and Birth Defects Correspondending to Wounds on Deceased Persons," by Ian Stevenson, Journal of Scientific Exploration, Vol. 7, No. 4, pp 403-410, 1993.
Life Before Life by Jim B. Tucker, St. Martin's Griffin, First Ed., 2008.

Thirteen: The Phenomenon of Animal Reincarnation – Their Potential through Our Eyes

Dr. Bruce Goldberg, personal correspondence to the author, 2012.
"Do We Love Our Dogs More Than People," by Claire Suddath, Time Magazine, 2009:
www.time.com/time/nation/article/0,8599,1888304,00.html
Dr. Bruce Goldberg, recorded interview with the author about animal reincarnation and the IBE state, 2012:
www.drbrucegoldberg.com.

REFERENCES

"Are Animals Soul Contracts, Pets Past Lives, Animal Afterlife part of the Reincarnation process after Pet Loss?" By Brent Atwater, adapted from Animal Reincarnation, Everything You Always Wanted to Know. Just Plain Love Books, 2011.

The Edgar Cayce Companion – A Comprehensive Treatise of the Edgar Cayce Readings. Compiled by B. Ernest Frejer. A.R.E. Press. Fourth printing, 1998.

Fourteen: Exploring Non-Physical Realms in the Out of Body State

"Sabreena's Story," as told to the author, circa 1990.

Journeys Out of the Body by Robert Monroe. Doubleday, 1971.

Adventures Beyond the Body by William Buhlman. HarperOne, 1996.

The Secret of the Soul by William Buhlman. HarperOne, 2001.

William Buhlman, recorded interview with the author about the out of body experience, 2012.

Fifteen: Navigate the Shift with Behavior Modification

"A Fuller View, Buckminster Fuller's Vision of Hope and Abundance for All", R. Buckminster Fuller, 1983.

REFERENCES

Sixteen: Want Change? Break Your Routine

The author's personal account of "the law of attraction" through the visualization process. (note, author does not make any claims that this process proves the existence of manifestation through non-material means but does illustrate strong evidence of same.)
Paul D. MacLean on the reptilian brain/complex. Various resources including: http://center-for-nonverbal-studies.org/basal.htm, https://en.wikipedia.org/wiki/Triune_brain , et al.

Seventeen: How to Manifest – Let's Get to the Heart of the Matter

The Secret (documentary), various artists/contributors, including Lisa Nichols. Prime Time Studios, 2006.
The Power of Now by Eckhart Tolle, New World Library, 2004.
The Power of Positive Thinking by Norman Vincent Peale. Fireside Books, 1952.
Think and Grow Rich by Napoleon Hill (original publication, 1937), reissued by Wilder Publications, 2008.
As a Man Thinketh by James Allen. (originally publication, 1903), reissued by Adams Media, 2012.
Institute of HeartMath, Boulder Creek, CA: www.heartmath.org.
Howard Martin, excerpted from a recorded interview with the author, February 2013.

Eighteen: Steps to Make Heart-Based Visualization More Effective

The author's personal account of "the law of attraction" through the visualization process. (note, author does not make any claims that this exercise proves the existence of manifestation through non-material means, but does illustrate strong evidence of same.)

Nineteen: Mapping Manifestation through the Dreamscape

The Quantitative Study of Dreams, Adam Schneider and G. William Domhoff, Univ. of California, Santa Cruz – DreamResearch.net: www2.ucsc.edu/dreams/FAQ/.

The Secret History of Dreaming by Robert Moss, New World Library, 2009.

A personal account as told to the author regarding "dreaming of law school and copyright award…," 1993.

Kelly Sullivan Walden, interviewed by George Noory, Coast to Coast AM. *Harnessing Your Dreams*, April 30, 2013.

Twenty: Sensing Reality from the Imaginal Realm

Mundus Imaginalis, or the Imaginary and the Imaginal by Henri Corbin, 1964: www.hermetic.com/moorish/mundus-imaginalis.html.

A dialogue between Penney Peirce and the author on the "Imaginal Realm." 2013.

Twenty-One: Feeling Your Way into the New World

Carlos Barrios, from *The Mystery of 2012 – Predictions, Prophecies and Possibilities* by Gregg Braden (and other contributors). Sounds True, Incorporated, 2009.

Beyond 2012 "Visual Meditation" originally published in the spoken word version of Conscious Musings by Alexis Brooks, Higher Journeys, 2012.

Twenty-Two: Not So Fast – Practice What You Preach!

The Synchronicity Highway – Exploring Coincidence, the Paranormal, & Alien Contact by Trish & Rob MacGregor, Crossroad Press, 2013.

All quotes listed as by "the author" are original by Alexis Brooks.
Some of the writings included in this volume have been previously published but adapted and/or expanded for the express purpose of this book.

Cover design by Justin Novelline:
justin@ornothing.com

Cover photography by Salwa Galal:
isis4beauty@gmail.com

About the Author

Alexis Brooks is a journalist, essayist and researcher within the metaphysical, spiritual and new thought genre.

A former media executive and commercial copywriter for mainstream television and radio broadcast outlets, Alexis now hosts a radio show on alternative news site Conscious Life News: *Conscious Inquiry with Alexis Brooks,* in which she interviews some of the most renowned experts in the fields of metaphysics, spirituality, new science and related subjects.

For over a decade, Alexis' work has appeared in both print and online including: Spirit of Change Magazine, Wisdom Magazine, Fate Magazine and on popular alternative websites like, Conscious Life News and LightWorkers World.

Her blog, Higher Journeys, features articles and essays on cutting edge subjects within the metaphysical genre.

Alexis lives in the Boston, MA area with her husband Derek.

Visit the author's web site at: www.higherjourneys.com

To purchase the original version of Conscious Musings (A Collection of Contemplations about Life and Potentiality) in spoken word format visit:
www.amazon.com/dp/B00ATHGW42